Sasanian Jewry and Its Culture

A Lexicon of Jewish and Related Seals

Sasanian Jewry and Its Culture

A Lexicon of Jewish and Related Seals

DANIEL M. FRIEDENBERG

Introduction by Norman Golb

UNIVERSITY OF ILLINOIS

URBANA AND CHICAGO

c 5 4 3 2 1

∞ This book is printed on acid-free paper.

Library of Congress Cataloging-in-Publication Data

Friedenberg, Daniel M.
Sasanian Jewry and its culture : a lexicon of Jewish and related seals / Daniel M. Friedenberg ; introduction by Norman Golb.
p. cm.
Includes bibliographical references and index.
ISBN 978-0-252-03367-4 (cloth : alk. paper) 1. Jewish seals (Numismatics)—Iraq. 2. Seals (Numismatics)—Iraq. 3. Babylonia—Seal. 4. Coins, Jewish—Iraq. 5. Coins, Sassanid—Iraq. 6. Jews—Iraq—Babylonia—Social life and customs.
I. Title.
CD5348.F75 2008
929.90935—dc22 2008035621

This book is dedicated
to the brilliant
scholarship of Professor Shaul Shaked

Contents

Seals of the Human Figure

Seals of Animals and Other Life Forms

Seals of Family Devices

Miscellaneous and Dubious Seals

Fantasy Seals on the Theme of the Binding of Isaac

Acknowledgments

Text Reviews: Professor Norman Golb
The University of Chicago, U.S.A.
Professor Shalom Sabar
Hebrew University, Jerusalem, Israel

Photography: Doron Boness, Tel Aviv, Israel

General Notes

1. Neither measure of depth is included nor the drilling method because both are extraneous to the analysis.

2. There is no distinction made between seal stones and finger rings for the same reason. All may be considered stamp seals.

3. The descriptions are taken from casts or photographs received of casts rather than from matrices unless indicated otherwise.

4. The Shaked numbers refer to his definitive article, "Jewish Sasanian Sigillography," in *Au Carrefour des Religions: Mélanges offerts à Phillipe Gignoux*, Res Orientales VII (Leuven, 1995), pp. 239–56. Shaked published several of these seals in previous publications (see bibliography, 1977 and 1981); wherever there is a duplication of material, they are not cited in the various bibliographies.

5. The *lulab* (palm branch) and *etrog* (citron) were ritual objects used at the Feast of Tabernacles. As this Jewish festival commemorated the dwelling of the Israelites in tents during their stay in the wilderness, it became by extension the main feast of the Temple. Thus, these two objects came to symbolize the Temple and national redemption. It is significant that they are a predominant element on Sasanian Jewish seals.

6. Christian and Zoroastrian seals, as well as those of uncertain background, are also described and illustrated despite the basic subject dealing with Jewish seals because they show a certain Sasanian communality of symbols and, in various cases, their similar roots in earlier history. This is especially true of seals depicting biblical subjects. In such cases the difference will be highlighted.

7. When references are taken from the seminal work of Judith Lerner, *Christian Seals of the Sasanian Period* (Istanbul, 1977), they are quoted verbatim though errors have been found. These are probably printing errors rather than those of the author.

8. The ending Hebrew letters א and ה are sometimes transliterated as *a, ah,* and *ha.* To conform throughout the author has translated as *a,* though in few cases the regular common use is retained.

9. Modern Persian place names are given in conventional anglicized forms. Hebrew names in seal titles are given in conventional forms and then phonetically. Accepted proper names are used rather than those more technical, *for example*, "Turks" rather than "Ottomans."

10. All seals are illustrated 1:1 or contact size unless indicated otherwise.

Sasanian Jewry and Its Culture

A Lexicon of Jewish and Related Seals

Introduction

Observations on the Jews of the Sasanian Empire

NORMAN GOLB

A tradition related in the historically valuable *Epistle* of Sherira Gaon states that when, during the years of strife in mid-seventh-century Iraq, Ali ibn Abi Talib arrived with Muslim forces at the gates of Firuz Shabur, a delegation of ninety thousand Jews went forth from the city under the leadership of Mar Rab Isaac, who paid him homage and who was greeted by the caliph in congenial manner. Another source, relating a similar tradition, asserts that it was Isaac alone who sallied forth, and that the Jewish inhabitants of the city at that time numbered ninety thousand.

This figure cannot be easily dismissed, for Jewish communities large and small densely populated Sasanian Babylonia and remained numerically important for centuries after the Arab conquest. Muqaddasi, for example, remarks at the great size of Sura, and Ibn al-Qifti writes that most of the inhabitants of Sura and Nahr-Malka were Jews. Muqaddasi likewise states that the Qasr ibn Hubaira (whose present-day ruins lie to the south of Sura) was "a large city with beautiful markets and containing many weavers and Jews." The rabbinic academy of Sura alone counted over a thousand students a year in its heyday. The known cities of Jewish population in Iraq during Sasanian times included not only academic centers such as Nisibis, Nehardea, Pum-Beditha (al-Anbar), Sura, Narach, Pum-Nehara, and Mahuza, but commercial and river-trade hubs as well. On the Tigris, for example, the most notable of these were Samarra, Ukbara, Bosra, Ba'aquba, Naharwan, Messene, Kashkar, and Hormshir (Ahwaz). On the Euphrates were cities of no lesser importance, such as Raqqa (Nicephorium), Dura (-Europos), Anah, Hadita, Hit (= Ihi Dekira, Ikra), the aforementioned Firuz Shapur, Borsif, Mata Mehasya, and already mentioned Qasr ibn Hubairah, Kafri, and Kufa. On the Sarsar canal stood an important town of that name, and on the Nahar Malka canal could be found a city likewise so named, both located in fertile territory heavily peopled by Jewish communities. All of these localities constitute but a small portion of the hundreds of places (a goodly number still unidentified) of Jewish settlement in Babylonia described by Adolph Neubauer and Jakob Obermeyer in their valuable writings on this subject. Jewish communities were of course located in other regions of the Sasanian Empire, but information is very sparse as to their size and cultural importance.

Many of the cities and towns of the Tigris and Euphrates regions, along with the abundant villages that surrounded them, could be reached by east-west canals that in turn supported a rich agricultural industry including the activities of countless Jewish farm communities. Indeed, the conclusion to be gained from a study of the Babylonian Talmud and the responsa of the indigenous rabbinic authorities is that agricultural pursuits formed the main occupation of the Jews residing in Iraq's heartland. One of the several canals of the Basra region was, according to Ibn Serapion, named the "(River of) the Jews" (al-Yahud); of the three canals in the vicinity of Samarra, the "uppermost" one, according to the same author, was similarly named "al-Yahud." Jacob Mann in his early monograph "The Responsa of the Babylonian Geonim as a Source of Jewish History" has given us a rich account of the various areas of specialization and techniques of planting and harvesting that the Jews of Mesopotamia engaged in. They cultivated cereal crops and vineyards of various kinds, palm-plantations in great abundance, but also many varieties of fruit-trees, as well as flax and other non-comestibles that were then turned by them into fabrics sold both regionally and on international markets. In general, the available evidence indicates that Jews of Sasanian Babylonia engaged intensively in trade and commerce both within the empire itself and with trading partners in regions of the Byzantine Empire.

There can be no doubt that the Jews of the Sasanian Empire enjoyed relatively great internal stability. They were officially represented at the royal court by a dignitary known as the Resh Galuta (Head of the Diaspora or Exilarch), who in turn exercised political and economic jurisdiction over all of the Jewish communities of the Sasanian realm. In this way the collection of taxes, for the benefit of both the empire and the Jewish communal institutions, was systematically and peacefully accomplished. As the author of the present volume observes, it was in Babylonia that the brilliant Nehardean academician Mar Samuel formulated the dictum that "the law of the land is the law." By this expression of fidelity to the secular rulers, which has placed its stamp upon all subsequent Jewish history, the Sasanian communities were accorded full jurisdiction over their own internal affairs, whether of a religious or a secular nature. Thus Jewish courts of law—except during relatively brief intermittent periods of suppression—flourished throughout the country, and the legal and societal opinions of the Mesopotamian rabbinic masters were sought and propagated internationally. The academies of higher learning, housed in imposing buildings, likewise achieved great renown throughout the Jewish ecumene. In the third through sixth centuries, the records of debates within those schools were, little by little, gathered together and came to form the main substance of the Babylonian Talmud. It is from the pages of this multifaceted and ponderous work that virtually everything we know today about the Jews of the Sasanian Empire can be derived.

Yet—as the author of the present volume also notes—with the exception of the well-known Aramaic incantation bowls, there is virtually nothing of the physical remains of this populous communal society that survives intact today. No monumental buildings or identifiable ruins—of schools, law-courts, or synagogues—have survived from Sasanian times, nor any original wall inscriptions, biblical or extra-biblical scrolls, legal documents, or personal autograph letters, or artistic or ornamental products, or items of clothing, implements, and utensils, which could be legitimately attributed to these people and which might enable us to assess the salient characteristics of their material culture. (The incantation bowls are very much akin to those written by native Mandaeans of the swamp-districts, and merely reflect, in language often repeated from one bowl to the next, superstitious beliefs and practices shared by illiterate or semiliterate inhabitants of the region.)

Given these circumstances, it is altogether noteworthy that various stamp seals of the Jews of the Sasanian Empire have survived intact and can be found today in both private and public collections around the world. These delicate objects, with their various depictions of human figures, of fauna, and of ceremonial motifs, strike one instantly by the high quality of their execution and the variety of their artistic nuances. Although it cannot be determined from what particular places in the empire they derive, it is nevertheless clear that, in often surprising ways, they portray the Jewish face of Sasanian civilization and point to the interpenetrability of the cultural mode of expression that characterized it.

The present publication of these seals, now all brought together in a single volume, thus adds a new dimension to our understanding of the Jewish community of the Sasanian Empire, while at the same time enriching our knowledge of the Sasanian stamp seal as revealed by publications of A. G. H. Bivar, Richard Frye, Phillipe Gignoux, and other scholars. The author of the present volume, who is Curator Emeritus of Coins and Medals at the Jewish Museum of New York, has distinguished himself by his previous publications on those subjects, and deserves our praise for his noteworthy achievement in bringing the present volume to fruition.

1 A Brief Historical Review

In 226 C.E. Ardashir, a Persian satrap or subordinate ruler, rebelled against the Parthian Empire, which extended from the Euphrates River in Babylonia east to the Indus River in India. Ardashir founded a new dynasty called the Sasanidae or Sasanians. He then added Armenia to this empire and put under tribute the Punjab in northwest India, as well as making Zoroastrianism the official religion of Persia.

Ardashir's son Shapur waged war against Rome and expanded west. For the next century a series of conflicts with Rome moved eastward and westward the size of the Sasanian Empire up to the reign of Shapur II, who stabilized the western frontier at the Euphrates River by defeating the Romans and driving them from Mesopotamia in 363 C.E. Wars with Rome and Byzantium went on until the last of the Sasanian kings, Yazdagird III, was defeated by the Arabs around 640 C.E.[1] Persia then became part of the Caliphate and the Zoroastrian religion was gradually absorbed into Islam.

This vast expanse of Persian history is little known by historians and even less by the general public. The cultural bias of Christians naturally draws them to Rome and its Byzantine cousin. And this is true of Jews as well because the rise of Ashkenazi Jewry tipped their interest in the same direction. Yet it must not be forgotten that the eastern Jews in this period, as well as for many centuries thereafter, were far more numerous and influential than the European and North African Jews.

Though the Babylonian Talmud might be considered the spine of Judaism after the Bible, it was written in a culture for which almost no Jewish relics remain. Next door in Palestine, though the Jews by this time were far fewer in number than in Mesopotamia, synagogue remains, tombs, mosaic floors, lead and stone bone boxes, oil lamps and other pottery, glassware, and jewelry are quite common. Many show Jewish symbols. None of this is found in Babylonia and eastern Persia despite the greater Jewish population.[2]

Research reinforces this puzzle. The important synagogue of Dura-Europos must be excluded. Situated on the Euphrates, it was repeatedly taken by the Parthians and then lost to the Romans until the city was conquered and sacked by the Sasanians in 256 C.E. The paintings date to 244/245 C.E. Their style is Eastern Hellenistic with much Parthian influence but does not depict Sasanian culture.[3]

We know from written records of another synagogue, Shaf Ve-Yativ, in Nehardea, a city in Mesopotamia that had a large Jewish population. This synagogue went back before Sasanian times as well.[4] A third-century synagogue was unearthed in Palmyra,[5] an area which, though under Sasanian influence from time to time, was not considered part of the empire. Ernst E. Herzfeld, the renowned Iranian scholar who explored the subject (1935), wrote of a tomb in Hamadan thought to be that of Esther. Herzfeld fixed it by style as the tomb of Queen Shūshāndokht (of which more later) and not that of Esther. In fact, in his later work (1941) there is no mention of any Jewish ruins: "Jewish" and "Hebrew" are not even in the index. A more recent study of the so-called tomb of Esther at Hamadan states that "though Jews have set pilgrimages to the shrine [at Hamadan] during the Festival of Purim for centuries, it is important to note that no extensive archaeological or historical research has been conducted to prove that the grave within the shrine is that of Esther."[6] The shrine itself was probably built around the seventeenth century, and was expanded and renovated in 1971.

No letters of exchange between the Babylonian and Palestinian religious academies of Sasanian times exist. Such writing can be inferred from the Talmudic prescript that scholars should only settle in places where there were professional scribes called "Lavlarim"; and there are references in the Talmud to written communications. But oral dispatch was the usual vehicle by which the rabbis shared thoughts. It was only in the eighth century, after the Arab conquest, that written inquiries (*She'elot*) were sent to Babylonia from the Diaspora and were answered by responsa (*Teshuvot*). These Hebrew and Aramaic papers from the later period—almost all from the Genizah (a depository for used sacred books and papers) in an attic of a synagogue of Old Cairo—are invaluable. But the earlier period is a blank. The only account of the installation of the exilarch (head of the Exile) and the customs of the Babylonian Talmudic academies was written by Nathan ha-Bavli, but this account comes much later.

There are two exceptions to this void of material relics. The first is what are called magic bowls or devil trap bowls. These bowls reflect the deep belief in devils or demons, often reflected in the Babylonian Talmud. The second is seals, almost all signet rings. In both bowls and seals the names, symbols, devices, and images—how like or unlike the objects are to similar Sasanian objects—pierce a peephole into a culture that seems to have faded without material trace. But to understand these artifacts a brief overview of Jewish society in Mesopotamia during this period is required.

The earlier Sasanian kings treated the Jews with justice and respect, a continuation of Parthian policy. Neusner states he could find no hostility or any evidence of Jewish persecution from the time of Ardashir I, except for a brief period at the start of his realm, to the reign of Yazdagird II, some two hundred years, that is, to the middle of the fifth century.[7] Official policy was to accept docile and hardworking minorities as subjects with equal rights before the law. As did the Turks later, the Sasanian rulers encouraged rich merchants and persons with special skills to settle in the Sasanian Empire. Widengren claims that Yazdagird 1 (399–420) married the daughter of Mar Zutra, the then-reigning exilarch.[8] Her name was Shoshen-duxt (a combination of the Hebrew *shoshan*, or lily, with the Pahlavi *duxt*, or daughter), now spelled Shoshandukht (or Shūshāndokht). This, according to Herzfeld, was the origin of the tie between her tomb and the name of Esther. Neusner, however, feels this is not likely, for rabbinical tradition makes no mention of such a marriage. It is certain, however, that the earlier neo-Sasanian kings marked Jewish leaders with special favor.

This policy was rent by Yazdagird II (438–457) after a few years in power, and the persecution was worse under his son Peroz, continuing from after 455 until 484. The reason was the growing influence on the kings of the Zoroastrian priests, the magi (priests) or *mowbads*, who began to feel menaced by Christian and Manichean conversion. The religious repression that resulted affected Jews as well as Christians and crippled state policy.

The internal strife in the royal family over the throne in the last century and a half of Sasanian rule weakened the state as well. Though some later rulers went back to a more tolerant religious policy, the continual family feuds led to civil wars. The Byzantines nibbled at the western and northern frontiers. The century of wars that began in 527 drained both states, and king followed king in very short order. Ten Sasanian kings in twelve years were raised to the throne by the competing factions at the end. The Arabs, seeing their chance, struck and in a brief time wiped out the kingdom. During the first half of the Sasanian epoch, however, and for intervals afterwards it was a happy lull for Judaism.

The Sasanian tolerance was smart politics. After Constantine (307–337), the first Christian Roman emperor, the Jews were viewed as allies while Christians were thought to lean toward Rome-Byzantium. Judaism at this period had given up conversion as policy[9] while the Sasanian Christians began to make inroads into the Iranian nobility. The Babylonian rabbis even accepted, despite the prohibition of sale of arms to gentiles, Jewish commerce in weapons because the Sasanians "defend us."[10] Since the Jews were concentrated in Babylonia along the western edge of the empire facing the Christian foe, favoring them was also good state politics. Many Jews were wealthy, for they profited from their position on both sides of the contested western frontier, especially in the very important silk trade. And often being rich they could lend money or bribe in order to escape oppression.

The legal position of Judaism was also more favorable under the Persians in the earlier years. State policy was not to interfere with internal Jewish religious activity, and the communities had autonomy. State taxes were reasonable compared to Rome's. The Sasanians usually imposed a single community tax based on the number of persons, which often led to an organized exodus upon news the tax collector was due; when too severe, a few rich men assumed the greater part. And the fertile land of Babylonia made taxes livable. The envy of Palestinians for the low cost of living in Babylonia is known from stories of the period.

During the third and fourth centuries the center of gravity of Jewish life gradually moved east from Palestine. The inflation, heavy taxes, and growing rigidity of Rome in its decline pushed this movement. Isfahan and Susania in the interior of Iran now saw large Jewish settlements spring up. And in the region of Ctesiphon (Tisfun), the neo-Persian capital of Babylonia not so far from the Roman frontier, many cities had a Jewish majority. It is recorded that at Maḥoza, overwhelmingly Jewish, the question arose as to whether the gates in the city wall should have *mezuzot*.[11] The result of this movement eastward was the diminished importance of the Palestinian patriarchy and its religious schools. The Byzantine rulers were also more religiously intolerant in this period and only the patriarch at Tiberias managed to survive in Palestine.

The Sasanian social structure was a caste system. The king lorded over the nobility. The priests and the bureaucracy bowed to the nobles. And these in turn dictated to the urban and rural masses. The Jewish social order followed suit. The Jewish leader was called *resh galuta*, from the Aramaic, meaning Head of the Exile, more commonly referred to as Exilarch. The exilarchs were descendants of the House of David and acknowledged as the same by the Babylonian Jews as well as the Sasanian rulers, who confirmed but did not choose them. Fourth in rank to the king, the exilarchs were treated with respect by the monarch and nobles.

From Mar Huna (ca. 212–297) in the time of the patriarch Judah I in Palestine the sequence of the exilarchs can be clearly traced until the eleventh century in an unbroken chain. Supreme judges of the Jewish communities in both civil and criminal cases or through hand-picked judges, the exilarchs were wealthy from income due to extensive land holdings as well as presents. With arbitrary power, they were often arrogant and given to violent deeds—indeed a mirror of their Sasanian overlords. Some, however, united with their power authority as teachers of the law. The rabbinic ruling "The law of the government is law" created a modus vivendi between them and the Persians.

The rabbis, who often doubled as district magistrates, were subject to the exilarchs. Tension developed, however, because the Davidic ancestry of the exilarchs did not depend on study of the law and the rabbis saw themselves as sole masters of the Oral Law. They thus disputed the exilarchic right to control and tax them. Backed however by the Sasanian kings (as mimic of their own social structure) the exilarchs closely watched the religious academies to assure their dependence.

The academies as the arbiters of Jewish law were led by these rabbis, called *amoraim* (from the Aramaic *amar*, speak)—thus by extension meaning to explain or interpret—known from the third to the sixth centuries. They lectured and commented on the Mishnah, already completed ca. the start of the third century in Palestine. Their work crystallized in the Gemara, which is the discussions by the *amoraim* on the Mishnah. Though over three thousand are known, it is apparent from the names that they too were a small oligarchy: sons and grandsons and sons-in-law are repeatedly referred to, as were in many cases their close relations to the exilarchs. The work of the amoraic teachers was finished with the final form of the Babylonian Talmud, usually considered completed in 499, by the unity of the Mishnah and Gemara.

Though overlapping in the sixth century, the *savoraim* (sometimes spelled *severaim*) rose for a brief period after the *amoraim*. Meaning in Hebrew "those who theorize or opine," thus called reasoners, the *savoraim* were scholars competent to make private but not authoritative judgments. Flourishing between 500 and 570, they completed the arrangement of the Babylonian Talmudic texts and, to make the sacred scripture more accessible to the less learned, introduced vowel points into the Hebrew Bible. Unlike the numerous *amoraim*, few of their names are recorded.

Both the *amoraim* and the *savoraim* were succeeded by the *geonim* (Excellencies), the formal title of the heads of the academies from the end of the sixth to the middle of the eleventh centuries. Descent was a big factor here too and, appointed by the exilarchs, six or seven families dominated their ranks. For example, at the academy of Sura, three families held the position for two hundred years. Most were what we would call political appointments to assure tight control on the part of the exilarchs. The geonic system developed at the end of Sasanian rule and is known mainly from Arab times. Though several thousand names are recorded, their renown is little: with the completion of the Babylonian Talmud, the function of the academies was to teach and not innovate.

2 The Jewish Academies

The top source for our knowledge of the Jews in the Sasanian Empire is through the religious academies which, forming and teaching the sacred texts, were the center of Jewish life. They can be briefly described.

THE NEHARDEA ACADEMY. Nehardea, the main Jewish settlement in Babylonia, was located at the junction of the Malka River with the Euphrates. The Nehardea Academy was elevated from a small school to great reputation by a very learned Jewish scholar named Samuel, also called Mar Samuel.

Mar Samuel (ca. 177–257), born in Nehardea, went to Palestine as a young man and studied under the patriarch Judah I before returning home. Noted also as an astronomer, Mar Samuel was an *amora* as well as district magistrate of Nehardea and was on friendly terms with the high nobility and king.

This was the period when the Parthians lost their empire to the Sasanians. Then, in 261 (though there are some arguments as to the precise date), Nehardea was sacked by Palmyrene forces. Because of this sack the Nehardea Academy was transferred to Maḥoza on the Tigris, near the site of Baghdad, but it never recovered its glory, ceding to the academies of Sura and Pumbedita.

THE SURA ACADEMY. Located on Lake Sura, this academy was founded by Abba b. Aibu, known more popularly as Abba Arika ("the Tall"). Like Mar Samuel, he had studied under Judah I in Palestine. His devoted students simply called him Rav, that is, master or teacher in Aramaic, a name that in time came to be applied to rabbis ordained in the Babylonian schools. His dates are usually considered from 220 to 247.

The exilarch and *amora* Mar Huna, referred to before, followed Abba Arika and was regarded as the foremost religious head in Babylonia. Due to his authority the Sasanian Jews became completely independent of Judaea, his well-known statement being "We consider being in Babylonia just the same as being in the Holy Land."[1]

Few of the *amoraim* from Sura stand out in history. The best known are Hisdai, then Rabbah b. Huna, and finally Mar b. Ashi, in whose time the compilation of the Talmud was completed.

The Pumbedita Academy. This academy rose at the same time as Nehardea but had a much longer history. The Pumbedita Academy was located a short distance from Sura. From 299 to 309 Pumbedita was headed by Huna b. Ḥiyyā. Shortly thereafter came Joseph b. Ḥiiyyā, 330 to 333. The *amora* Ḥiiyyā b. Abba, also born in Babylonia, was sent home by the Palestinian patriarch Judah III to raise a tax for his support. Known earlier, ca. 250, was an *amora* at Sura and Nares with the name Ḥiiyyā b. Rav. The similarity of names, including those from other academies, illustrates the inner structure of these Jewish oligarchies.

The academies of Sura and Pumbedita continued to dominate Jewish life in Babylonia for the next eight centuries.

The Nares Academy. This was a new academy founded near Sura. Well known was the founder, the *amora* Papa b. Ḥanan (ca. 300–375). The Nares Academy, like that at Mahḥoza, successor to Nehardea, never attained great distinction in regard to its teachers.

The shift of Jewish life from Palestine to Babylonia is reflected in the importance of the Babylonian Talmud over the Jerusalem Talmud, as well as in the long-lasting academies with their outstanding leaders. It was a shift fully backed by the exilarchs, locking in their power, and also by the Sasanian monarchs who—for the same reason they supported the Nestorian Christians—agreed to any measure that reduced reliance on Rome-Byzantium.

That this great culture, with the teeming Jewish cities of Mesopotamia, with famous academies and synagogues, and with a rich commercial life, has left few traces seems incredible. Possibly someday, when a more civil and tolerant system comes to Iraq, the present heir to Babylonia, digs will unearth, as they have in Israel, extensive ruins.[2] As of now, however, aside from the soaring words of the Babylonian Talmud, we must mainly depend on the magic bowls and seals to decipher what remains.

3 Jewish Names on Sasanian Seals

It is exceedingly difficult to identify specific Jews, particularly the top individuals such as exilarchs and *amoraim*, from the few Sasanian seals known. The reason is that the same names were used over and over without reference to position or other identification. These are personal seals merely showing a name, often only one name. This was common practice at the time; non-Jews, even in high position, did not necessarily indicate a title or rank on their seals. Also, unlike later Western medieval seals, there were relatively few standard devices or symbols relating a person's name to a specific family or place in the social structure except such obvious ones as crowns for kings.

This can be shown by examples taken from the names known from Jewish Sasanian seals.

There are seals for an Abbua, an Abb, and an Abba b. Malka.[1] Abba is a common name in this period; it derives from the Aramaic for Father, an address of esteem. Mar Samuel's father, also an *amora* at Nehardea, was Abba b. Abba. An Abba was an exilarch from 350 to 370; an *amora* named Abba is known from 360 at Pumbedita (as mentioned, since some exilarchs were *amoraim* as well, this may be the aforementioned exilarch). Another with this same name besides those not referred to before at the academies was Abba b. Jeremiah, an *amora* at Sura and Nares ca. 270.

There appear to be seals for Hunā b. Nathan (No. 9) and Huna b. Samuel (No. 33). Huna as a name was even more common than Abba, and appears as well on magic bowls from the period. In the Babylonian Talmud there are no less than sixty persons of that name mentioned. From 170 (preceding the Sasanian conquest) to 508, a series of exilarchs were simply called Huna I to Huna VI. Similar to Abba, the name Huna was common to *amoraim* from the academies of Sura and Pumbedita: they were often the exilarchs as well, notably at Pumbedita. Rav Huna, an early exilarch, may have been one of those numbered without further clarification. A second R. Huna, living at the end of the third century, was an *amora* at Sura and a top scholar contributing to the Babylonian Talmud. His son, Rabbah b. Huna (309–322), was also an *amora*. Other *amoraim* with this name were Huna b. Joshua, known from 370 at Mahḥoza; Naḥman b. Huna, who died in 455; and Ravina b. Huna (470–499).

As referred to above, the seal of Hunā b. Nathan (No. 9) seems to match a known person from history, an exilarch and *amora* of the late fourth century. Also those for Isaac b. Adda (No. 28) and, again as noted, Huna b. Samuel (Seal No. 33) are names known from this period.

There are seals for a Joseph and a Joseph b. Nata. Joseph b. Ḥama was an *amora* around 330 at Maḥoza; Joseph b. Ḥiiyyā, as mentioned, was an *amora* at Pumbedita from 330 to 333; also R. Jose (Joseph) from around 460 to 500.

As for the seals of Samuel and Samuel b. Isaac Rabba (or Rava), there was an *amora* named Samuel at Nehardea from 220 to 250. Also Samuel b. Shilat is known from around 270 at Sura and Nares. A Mari b. Samuel is likewise mentioned.

Mar in Aramaic was an honorific title, translated as Master or Lord, degenerating in later Hebrew to the more simple Mr. Mari probably meant My Master, as Rab (or Rav) became Rabbi. Mari is also the name of an ancient city on the Euphrates east of Palmyra (Tadmor) and, like Malka, may have given its name to individuals from that city.

As to the honorary title Mar, as, e.g., preceding Huna, it was common to many exilarchs who, however, usually added their names afterward. There were all kinds of combinations employing this name. A well-known exilarch was Mar Zutra I, whose son Huna Mari, also an exilarch, was executed (469/470) for disobedience to the monarch. An exilarch named Huna Mar has been described as living shortly after the date. The exilarch Mar Zutra II followed his father Huna in power from 488 to 508. Again showing confusion as to dates, it is likewise claimed that Mar Zutra, rebelling against the Zendist communist philosophy of King Kobad (which included women as common property and thus was opposed as well by Christians), was executed around 520, while his posthumous heir, also named Mar Zutra, escaped to Judaea. The repetition of these names, often without mentioning the full name of the son as well as the father, has led to a history that must be approached with caution. Jacob Neusner, referring to the various known lists showing striking divergences, states, "Yet I think we may take as fact the assignment of various sages to the several schools, even though why one school should be subsumed under another is obscure."[2]

This is true of the exilarchs as well. Even when we are quite certain of the facts, name confusion is apparent. For example, after the reign of Chosru II (590–628)—also spelled Khosro—the academies at Sura and Pumbedita, closed during the Sasanian civil wars, were reopened. Mari b. Mar succeeded Ḥanan at Pumbedita while Mar b. Huna (609–ca. 620) was head at Sura. Here we see that Mar, an honorary title, seems to be used as a proper name; the relation of Mari as son of Mar is difficult to understand. It is true that when a full name is shown, that is, of son and father, we can take an educated guess. But none of these seals match in that sense any known persons from the period with the possible exceptions of those noted as well as certain less known Talmudic scholars mentioned by Shaked in his seal descriptions.

There are also inconclusive clues. When the name is mentioned without that of the father it is possible the person was so well known in the contemporary community—as in the case of the exilarchs named Huna—that the title might have been deemed sufficient. Furthermore, the use of Mar, sometimes before and sometimes after, such as Huna Mar or Mar Zutra, would almost surely indicate high position because the exilarchs used this title. This was also true in the Babylonian academies for Rav, probably indicating *amoraim*. Sometimes these sages fused their names, such as Rava for Rav Abba or Romi for R. Ammi. Thus, the implication would be that if seal names show Mar or Mari, or Rav or Rava, or Huna, these were seals of distinguished individuals, most likely religious. Indeed, prominent non-Jewish Sasanian persons, as shown on their seals, were often solely known by their titles, such as High Priest or High Judge. The use of a title rather than a proper name was not unusual in the ancient world. In Egypt the kings were often simply called Pharaoh instead of their names, out of reverence. As examples, the Pharaoh referred to by Abraham (Gen. 12:15–20) and the Pharaoh of Joseph (Gen. 40:2–23; 41:1–55) are unidentified; and even the Pharaoh of Exodus, though usually considered Ramesses the Great (1279–1213 B.C.E.), is only referred to by this title, simply meaning Great House in Egyptian.

Another possible key is the combination of *etrog* and *lulab* shown on Jewish seals, which would likely point to a religious figure rather than a merchant. It will be noted that, more than in any other category, the name-bearing seals showing this combination are those most closely linked with very important known Jewish religious leaders. One might even hazard a guess that the *lulab* and *etrog* shown on such seals were the official designation of such figures. Yet

Jewish tombstones of ordinary people in the European Diaspora often show these symbols (as well as the menorah, shofar, and jug for sacramental wine) simply to indicate that they were Jews. And it is likewise strange, given the long history of Jews linking their names to those of their fathers, that some of these seals show only one name.

We thus face the very difficult task of identifying just who the men owning these seals were though it is apparent that, as seal owners, they stood high in the hierarchy of Jewish Sasanian society. The difficulty can be further shown by quoting one sentence (b. Ber. 22b): "R. Papa, R. Huna b. R. Joshua, and Rava b. Samuel were eating together." The readers at that time knew who these men were but it is quite different some seventeen hundred years later.[3] When the same *amora* appears with a variant name in another context or two exilarchs or *amoraim* from different generations bear the same name, and indeed when certain of these names seem to have been transmitted incorrectly, the result is confusion.

There are clues from later times. In the period of the Omayyad caliphate following the Arab conquest Jewish institutions continued. A few seals from this period have been identified. That of Bustanai b. Ḥaninai showed a wasp or fly, reputedly because Bustanai, standing as a child in respect before the caliph, would not swat an insect stinging him. The caliph, impressed, made the boy exilarch. Several successive exilarchs supposedly used the same device on their seals. The seal of Ḥai b. Sherira, *gaon* at Pumbedita from 998 to 1038, had a lion as device, surely standing for his pride in being a descendant of the House of David.

Since these Jewish institutions flowed forward in tradition from the earlier Sasanian period, this would argue, as referred to before, that the *etrog* and *lulab* on a seal might stand for an exilarch, especially that showing the name Huna or Hunā, while the appearance of double wings below the bust would indicate a person with high standing concerning official relations to the nobility or monarch.

It should be emphasized that for every Jewish Sasanian seal we possess there are probably many hundreds lost. It is claimed that every time the mud shifts in the Bosphorus, Byzantine seals are found because personal seals, which no longer had a use after the merchant died, were thrown into the shore waters. References in medieval European documents from Germany also indicate similar large numbers of Jewish seals. Commercial or personal seals were thus discarded when no longer serving a function while a few seals of high Jewish figures such as exilarchs and the most prominent *amoraim* survived because they were so cherished.

4 The Nature and Function of Sasanian Seals

Sasanian seals are quite simple and naturalistic. The male portrait, the head almost always facing right and bearded, is one of the most common types for the highest echelon—kings, nobles, officials, magi—of Sasanian society. Female portraits also exist: one identifiable seal shows the widow of Yazdagird II, ca. 457. Among animals the most common portrayed is the lion, a tradition that long precedes this culture. Rams, goats, bulls, bears, and scorpions are depicted.[1] They may represent astrological themes as seen in the Zodiac, a theory strengthened by their not infrequent association with astral bodies such as stars and crescents. Another suggestion is that they might indicate the horoscopes of the seal owners, as was true later in Europe. Two other common motifs were the fire altar and the extended hand; the latter probably invoked the great Sky-God; while the fire altar surely addressed the supreme god, Ahura Mazda.

According to A. D. H. Bivar,[2] the rather rare Sasanian emblems or devices had their origin as cattle brands among the nomadic Iranians, and later came to indicate marks of ownership on other property as well, including insignia on battle armor. This led in turn to hereditary connotations in the highly structured Sasanian society, similar to emblems on shields in medieval Christianity. Some, though not all, of these emblems or devices incorporated letters of the Pahlavi alphabet and thus may be considered monograms. The cross also appears as a device on some Christian Sasanian seals. Both Jews and Christians, as well as a few somewhat similar Zoroastrian images, show The Binding of Isaac; while Christian Sasanians also show Daniel in the Lions' Den, itself an image—in another context—going back much farther in time.

Double wings, indicating royalty or priestdom, are probably based on those of the eagle, who can soar high in the sky to rest on mountain peaks, a dominant element in Zoroastrian religion. These double wings appear on the crowns of many of the Sasanian kings as shown on both coins and seals. Deriving earlier from Babylonian art, their origins relate to a parallel development in ancient Egypt with the image of the winged solar disk.

High, resting on mountaintops, is the abode of the gods. Also probably with roots in Mesopotamia, on the stele of Hammurapi's Code, the god Shamash, enthroned on a mountain, revealed to that king of Babylonia (ca. 2100 B.C.E.) the immutable law that must govern society. This is also expressed in the later Greek belief in gods living on Mount Olympus as well as in ancient Hebraic cultural themes possibly deriving from that of its predecessor, the storm-god in Canaanite texts. It is repeated several times in the Bible (Exod. 19:3; 19:16–20). In Exodus 24:15–18, we read that Moses went up the mountain to meet Yahweh; "The Glory of Yahweh took up dwelling on Mount Sinai." It has even been claimed, though disputed, that the root of the Hebrew word *Shaddai*, often translated as "Almighty" and often used on amulets, may mean "of the mountain," referring to the Divinity living high up in the mountains. Thus, the wings, the stars, the crescents, and even the mouflon, or wild mountain goat, take on specific meaning as Sasanian seal devices.

Common on these seals are plant elements, especially the rose and the tulip. Curiously, the pomegranate does not appear on any known Jewish Sasanian seals despite its ancient Jewish symbolism. Perhaps the reason is similar to the absence of the menorah despite its importance on contemporary Jewish objects in nearby Palestine.[3]

Just as *The Iliad* informs us of the gods and goddesses who lived on Mount Olympus, and the Bible tells us that Yahweh dwelled on Mount Sinai, so the study of syllography of the Late Bronze Age shows that almost two-thirds of the seal stones and rings depict animals similar to those shown on Sasanian seals, mainly lions and bulls. That the lion symbolizes power and majesty is underlined by the fact that the lion does not seem to be native to the Aegean but was probably brought to certain palaces as a gift.[4] The lion is shown on mosaics from Palestine in the Sasanian period. As an example, a sarcophagus in Catacomb 20 at Beth Shearim depicts confronting roaring lions; indeed, far earlier, among the stone carvings from the sanctuary at Hazor, fourteenth to thirteenth centuries B.C.E., there is a side figure of a roaring lion.

A significant percentage of Sasanian seals do not show names. They often constitute the authentication of office, secular or religious. For example, Khosro I (531–579) had four seals: that for the Revenue was engraved "Justice"; that for the Estates Department was engraved "Development"; that for the Council was engraved "Deliberation"; and that for the postal services was marked "Equity." Nor rarely do Sasanian seals show pious quotations, as do those of the contemporary Byzantine or later Islamic periods. This further supports the hypothesis that names like Abba or Huna were titles on Sasanian Jewish seals rather than individual names; or perhaps a combination of both functions.

There are certain other considerations that point to background. Despite the similarity of Sasanian seals to those of earlier Parthia, Parthian seals are so rare most such seals can automatically be assigned to the later Sasanian period. The Arsacid (Parthian) and Sasanian styles are not abruptly different, with Arsacid influence apparent, especially in the earlier period. Obviously, however, the use of Pahlavi script, Sasanian names, and/or offices confirm the difference between the two epochs. The matter is still tricky; a scholar as brilliant as Philippe Gignoux assigns certain seals considered Sasanian to the preceding Parthians.

There are two physical types of seals, seal stones and finger rings. All, however, may be considered stamp seals, for ring bezels were used for stamping as well. Size is the most important distinction. The largest seals are those of royalty, usually showing a portrait with an inscription giving the name and title. Richard N. Frye[5] considers thereafter that the smaller seals were official and only showed the name of the administrative provinces and the title of offices, not the specific name of the office holders. These seals belonged to the chief priest or magus of the city or district who certified the juridical decision or, in case of commerce, the goods for tax purposes, transit, or depot. The lesser-size seals belonged to the owner of the goods being sealed, while the smallest seals were those of witnesses. Frye states these suggestions are tentative but seem to best answer their purpose.

Joseph M. Upton[6] categorizes zeals more formally. The rulers and princes are identified by individual crowns, the principal officers probably by monograms, as under the Parthian rulers, while administrative seals bore the inscription of the office and its location, as indicated in the case of Khosro I. Upton emphasizes the importance of the Zoroastrian priesthood, shown by seals bearing the name of the office or temple, or in the case of their personal seals, the name of the magus as well. Though nowhere is it explicit because we have only the stone seals themselves (or very rarely, bronze ones), they must have been impressed into a wet lump of clay, which was stuck on strings that were wrapped around the document or letter. These had to be broken to open the communication, thus validating the contents. Collections still show traces of the impressions left by the strings that once attached them to the sealed objects.

J. M. Unvala[7] is in general agreement with Frye as to the relation of size to function. He states that packages of goods, either in transit or for depot, were sealed by state officials, and sometimes as well by the owners and witnesses, though the legality of the different seal types is not clarified. It would thus seem quite certain that almost all Sasanian Jewish seals being of the smallest type—at least those known—were used to witness documents. Unlike Jewish seals from late medieval Europe, they had no legal value in the larger community and merely attested other signatures, except possibly within the Jewish community itself.

Phyllis Ackerman[8] states that due to the great similarity of subjects, these smaller seals were probably not made to order but were simply seal-cutters' stock, sometimes with a name added. In Jewish seals, however, this seems not true because the seals showing The Binding of Isaac and those with the *etrog/lulab* combination have distinct differences in detail and therefore could not come from a common stock.

The function of monograms is still inconclusive. Monograms are shown as emblems on the casques of important nobles and high officials, some accompanied by legends and others not. They appear with the portraits of such officials as well as on rock carvings and these are considered badges of rank; they also appear on stucco ornaments. The opinion of A. D. H. Bivar has already been cited. Göbl[9] states the ribbon is a symbol of the wreath or garland of the government, similar to the crown. The knot he views as a double loop binding the owner to the state. He finds functional similarities between the Sasanian monograms and those of the late Byzantine era. However, Göbl concludes that the artistic intertwining or interlocking done by the engraver can in many cases never be deciphered. Whether these are clan or tribal devices, family emblems, or simply individual symbols, the only sure point is that monogram seals belong to the elite of Sasanian society.

Like the late Romans and Byzantines, as the bureaucracy grew, so did the number of seals. Site finds indicate their omnipresence in legal and commercial functions. In fact, Brunner[10] states that seals, together with coins, are the largest class of cultural artifacts surviving from the Sasanian Empire. Excluding coins, which are exclusively the issue of the state authority, as well as extant Jewish magic bowls, this is likewise true of the Jewish seals.

Herein lies their great importance for what they reveal of Jewish life, both religious and secular, in Sasanian society. A seal, as distinct from a standard religious text, mirrors much of local custom and belief. These seals often indicate a common lore shared by Jews, Christians and Zoroastrians. When, for example, the altar on which Isaac is to be sacrificed looks like a fire altar, this cultic reference to Zoroastrian worship tells us of Jewish assimilation into Sasanian civilization; indeed the *Aqedah* itself, considered so uniquely Jewish, is part of a larger common heritage. As God saved Isaac and provided a ram as substitute on the altar, so in Greek culture Artemis saved Iphigeneia at Aulis by snatching her away and putting a stag in her place on the altar.

The common depiction of lions, bears, and scorpions on such seals shows as well not only this assimilation but relates both societies to much older Near Eastern beliefs. The portrayal of the mouflon ties it to a common heritage of the worship of gods who live in inaccessible mountains. We can thus construct a series of societal beliefs of the Jew living under Sasanian rule and the relation of both to a common background extending from the Eastern Mediterranean to Mesopotamia from these small and seemingly insignificant seals.

Excluding those Sasanian Jewish seals that show the *etrog* and *lulab*, general collections of Sasanian seals plus those found *in situ* at Qasr-i Abu Nasr indicate clearly that if it weren't for the Hebrew letters, there would be no way to distinguish Jewish from non-Jewish Sasanian seals.[11] As Ernst E. Herzfeld states, "There was never, of course, a distinct Jewish or Christian art in these [Sasanian] lands; the general style of the various periods was simply followed."[12]

5 Old Testament Themes

The Binding of Isaac and Daniel in the Lions' Den

There are two Old Testament scenes shown on Sasanian seals, The Binding of Isaac and Daniel in the Lions' Den. They have provoked much scholarly controversy as to whether they are Christian or Zoroastrian rather than Jewish.

Earlier scholars identified The Binding of Isaac as being a Zoroastrian priest (magus) before a fire altar about to sacrifice a ram. But this has now been rejected because the figure to be sacrificed—whether seated, kneeling or lying on the altar, or floating above or beside the altar—is not a ram. Sometimes the body is indicated with realism, sometimes as a stick figure, other times as merely horizontal lines, but it is definitely meant to be human rather than that of an animal. Indeed on one seal a figure that may be identified as Isaac is portrayed sitting on a rock, which might be Mount Moriah. Other factors point to Christianity or Judaism. The hand of God or that of an angel, more clearly indicating the event, reaches down from above on several seals. The ram, though appearing in variant forms and positions, sometimes even omitted, is trapped or close to a bush or thicket. The bearded adult bears an uplifted knife close to the altar, often with head turned toward the ram or the hand extended from the sky. Thus, the combination of these features—the male lifting a knife, the smaller sacrificial figure, the ram, the bush or thicket, and the overhead hand—seems clearly to indicate that these seals refer to the

Old Testament story and not to another, whether Babylonian or Greek, or a sacrifice by a Zoroastrian magus.[1]

The sacrificial scene was much favored by Christians as a prefiguration of the crucifixion and salvation. Judith Lerner lists twenty-five examples.[2] More are known and several other examples not mentioned by Lerner—as well as later imitations—are illustrated in the following catalogue. Crosses on several back her opinion that they are Christian.

Despite this evidence, Rika Gyselen, a Sasanian seal expert, indicates great doubt as to whether any seeming Old Testament seals are Christian. The crosses, in her opinion, are a part of the tradition of Sasanian glyptic art unrelated to Christianity, and may be interpreted as four-pointed stars. She likewise points out that no such seals bear Syriac inscriptions, the script of the Monophysite and Nestorian churches. Curiously, one seal sometimes considered Sasanian, and illustrated in this work, bears a Latin inscription. The seal probably is late Roman rather than Sasanian. It might be added that the renowned Jewish Sasanian expert, Shaul Shaked, shared her doubt in his earlier writing.[3]

These eminent scholars were apparently not aware of a few *Aqedah* seals that bear in Hebrew letters a proper name. Assuming the letters were not added later, this evidence is irrefutable that Jews also employed the theme on their seals, though much less so than Christians. (See Nos. 12 and 13.) The writer thus shares the opinion of Judith Lerner that The Binding of Isaac seals are largely Christian, with, however, a few being Jewish.

The rejection of a Christian background is also extended by Gyselen when referring to the other seeming Old Testament theme shown on Sasanian seals, Daniel in the Lions' Den. She mentions two rare examples where the Pahlevi or Middle Persian inscriptions state "Confidence in the gods," as incompatible with the Christian faith in one God.[4] Gyselen likewise refers to their thematic similarity to the ancient oriental motif of the Tamer of Wild Animals or Master of Animals. She thus thinks that the Daniel theme might have a Judeo-Christian connotation, but "it would seem that the lapidaries had searched to underline that the persons, as Abraham, Daniel and the Master of Animals, belonged to a lengthy tradition . . . [and] that the Sasanian lapidary knew the scene that he engraved related to a religious and cultural patrimony which lost itself in the nights of time."[5]

This view is inconclusive. Unlike the earlier royal persons portrayed as lion tamers, the figure depicted as Daniel on this group of seals does not touch or hold the lions, which is true to the Biblical account. In Mesopotamian, Achaemenid, and Parthian art the heroes dangle or strangle the lions. Furthermore, instead of a figure, there is a cross on or over the altar (Nos. 16, 18, and

20). Usually lacking inscriptions, the evidence seems clearly to indicate that they represent Daniel in the Lions' Den and are Christian.

These two Old Testament themes are equally significant in Christian and Jewish iconography as representing divine deliverance in which Abraham and Daniel demonstrated their total faith and trust in God. The former, which also obviously is a prefiguration of the crucifixion, is far more common as a Christian seal type than the latter. Indeed, these Binding of Isaac Christian seals total more than all the known Jewish Sasanian seals put together; and as to the Daniel story, the only Jewish image usually referred to appears as a floor mosaic in the fifth- to sixth-century synagogue at Na'aran (Ain Duk), near Jericho.[6] It seems conclusive that the Sasanian Jews rarely used these religious imageries.

Oddly, the portrayals of Jonah thrown to the fish and the three Hebrews in the fiery furnace, which are similar examples of total faith and commonly shown on Christian objects from the same period,[7] do not appear in Sasanian glyptic art. Like the two Old Testament themes discussed, Jonah as a Christian representation is far more common than a Jewish one, probably because in Matthew 12:39–40 Jesus relates the Jonah story to his own death and resurrection.

Judith Lerner makes an interesting observation, namely that the choice by Christians of these two biblical themes goes beyond religious symbolism.[8] She states that their popularity might have been due to a similarity with traditional Sasanian motifs, that is, the worshipper before the altar and the hero between two lions, thus attesting to Christian national fidelity as a minority in the Sasanian Empire—for the Christians were far more suspect of lack of patriotism than the Jews because of their religious ties with hostile Byzantium and Rome.

In summary it may be stated that of the known Old Testament themes, the only ones shown on Sasanian seals seen by the writer are those of The Binding of Isaac and Daniel in the Lions' Den. Despite some scholarly opinion to the contrary these are indeed the subject matter of the seals and not similar stories from other cultures. The Binding of Isaac is the more popular of the two. The background on both of these themes is Christian rather than Jewish. There exist a few *Aqedah* seals with Hebrew names, which opens the possibility that some without such inscriptions may be Jewish as well. No known evidence indicates, however, that the seals portraying Daniel in the Lions' Den are anything other than Christian. In the cases where crosses are shown, and they are on both seal types referred to, it is the opinion of this writer that the weight of evidence indicates these are truly Christian crosses and not some other decorative element used in Sasanian glyptic art.

6 Description of Seals

SEALS OF THE *LULAB* AND *ETROG* (1–11)

1. Seal of Mari Son of Samuel

מרי בר שמואל
Mari bar Shmuel
15 × 13 mm
Matrix: Carnelian

Provenance: Catalogue Legrain of the University Museum, 1925: 361, No. 1048, pl. XLVIII, fig. 10.

Description: A *lulab* to right and an *etrog* to left. Inscription round, four large dots before, two large dots after.

Shaked Number and Remarks: Shaked 23. The final *yōd* in the first name may be an imperfection in the cutting. Possibly, due to this imperfection, the first name might be מרד or the Iranian name Mard. The name Mari, however, is widely attested; see Hyman (1964), III: 903ff.; and Albeck (1969), index s.v.

Author's Remarks: Though smudged, the writer agrees with the name Mari. The full name shown is of interest because of its close relation to Mar Samuel, the great *amora* of Nehardea. It may also be mentioned that seal cutters, for lack of space or aesthetic reasons, occasionally omitted certain letters or abbreviated words; the same thing is relevant among certain writers of antiquity, though in the latter case it is more likely ignorance.

Location: University Museum of the University of Pennsylvania, Philadelphia, B 5110.

Bibliography: *Encyclopaedia Judaica,* vol. II, col. 992.

2. Seal of Isaac Son of Papa

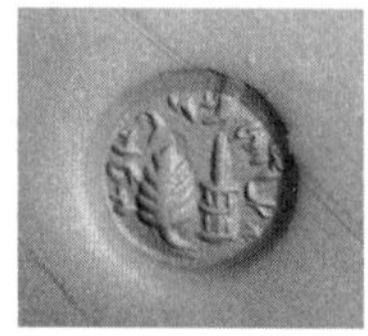

יצחק בר פאפא

Yitzḥāk bar Pāpā

13 mm diam.

Matrix: Carnelian

Description: A *lulab* to right and an *etrog* to left. Inscription round in sloppy letters.

Shaked Number and Remarks: Shaked 20. *Sefer ha-Eškol* includes the name Isaac bar Papa but this may be a scribal error. See Abraham of Narbonne, *Sefer-ha-Eškol* 1:160; Sherira Gaʾon, *Iggeret,* 1921: 180f.; and *Habdala de-Rabbi ʾAqiba* (Scholem [1980–81], 281).

Author's Remarks: Pāpā (sometimes spelled Pappa) is a very distinguished Jewish Sasanian name; as noted above, Pāpā b. Ḥanan founded a school at Naresh near Sura.

Location: National Museum of Denmark, Copenhagen, 9470.

3. Seal of Judah—Son of Abba

יהודה מ[...]א בר אבה

Yehuda [...] bar Abba

12 × 10 mm

Matrix: Red sardonyx

Description: A *lulab* to right and an *etrog* to left. Inscription round.

Shaked Number and Remarks: Shaked 2. The middle name, which starts with a *mēm*, is doubtful, possibly מדיא, Madayya. (If so, this could stand for a Mede, a person from Media, the region in western Persia.) The name Judah bar Abba is that of an *amora*; see Hyman (1964), II:553; it occurs three times in the Palestinian Talmud; see Kosovsky (1985), 22a (in Hebrew).

Author's Remarks: The letters of the middle name are so badly formed and positioned, there is a question as to whether they were originally there. Though there seem to be four letters, they might also be a misspelling or odd spelling of מָרא, which could be (like Mar or Mari, that is, My Lord) an honorific title; perhaps even מריא, or מריוא, one form of which Shaked suggests.

Location: Museum für Islamische Kunst, Staatliche Museen zu Berlin, V.A. 1531. Berlin, Germany.

Bibliography: Horn and Steindorff, No. 1531.

4. Seal of Abbua

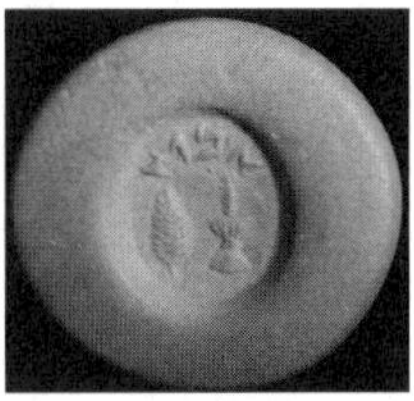

אבוא

Abbua

14 × 11 mm

Matrix: Violet-colored stone, probably hyacinth

Provenance: Former M. Marcus Collection; said to come from Iran.

Description: A *lulab* to right and an *etrog* to left, inscription above.

Shaked Number and Remarks: Shaked 21. Catalogued as אבוא the name may be a variant of the Talmudic name אבי״ (*abī* = my father), commonly read Abbaye. (Based on Joseph Naveh's reading).

Author's Remarks: The writer clearly sees the above spelling, Abbua. Abba is sometimes used as an epithet for God, and is also used as such in the Talmud. Jacob Neusner in *Israel and Iran in Talmudic Times* refers several times to an Abayye, a mid-fourth-century *amora* (see pp. 76, 85, and 146).

Location: Kadman Numismatic Pavilion, Eretz-Israel Museum, K-974-84. Tel Aviv, Israel.

Bibliography: Haaretz Museum (1984), p. 3.

5. Seal of Ahawa Son of Zachary

אחיה בר זכריה

Aḥawa bar Zachria

16 × 14 mm

Description: A *lulab* to right and an *etrog* to left. Inscription round, with the circle completed by a line of dashes ending in a small figure like a floret.

Shaked Number and Remarks: Shaked 10. The inscription might be the above or possibly Aḥiyya bar Zachariah. The small figure at the end of the dashes may be a stylized hand.

With variant spellings there are Talmudic scholars having similar names. The name אחיה is mentioned in an inscription from Dura Europos.

Author's Remarks: The inscription on this seal is an excellent example of the difficulty caused by writing certain letters in a very similar way on many of these seals: the *ḥēt* and the *hē*; the *wāw* and the *yōd*; and the *rēsh* and *dalet̲*—in this case the last *rēsh* even resembles a *lamed*, though this may be an imperfection. The writer accepts Shaked's reading for lack of a better one. To illustrate the difficulties in reading these seals, Gignoux ([1978], No. 8.4) saw the inscription as Parthian and deciphered it as Ābdād, son of Gul-dād.

Location: Cabinet des Médailles, Bibliothèque Nationale, Paris, 1972.1317.53.

Bibliography: Gignoux (1978), p. 65, pl. xxiv. 8.4.

6. Seal of Joseph

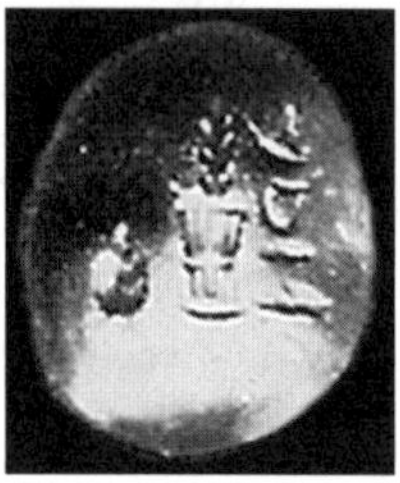
[Enlarged]

יוסף

Yosef

11.6 × 8.7 mm

Matrix: Amandine garnet

Description: A *lulab* to right, *etrog* to left. Inscription to extreme right.

Shaked Number and Remarks: Shaked 15. The seal comes from an unnamed collection in Iran. The inscription is read differently by Gignoux.

Author's Remarks: As above stated, the letters resemble each other closely on these Sasanian seals. Shaked reads the first letter as *yōd* followed by *wāw*. The two letters on closer scrutiny seem to be a *wāw* followed by a *yōd*. This, however, does not make sense as a name.

Location: Private collection.

Bibliography: Gignoux and Gyselen (1982), p. 147, 60.3, pl. XXV.

7. Seal Without Inscription

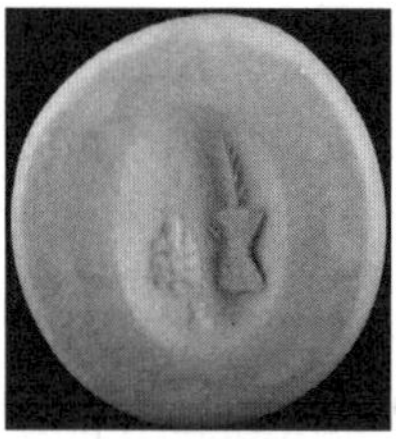

18.5 × 13 mm

Matrix: Blue glass

Provenance: Bought by dealer from Iran.

Description: A *lulab* to right, an *etrog* to left, beneath the *etrog* a small object like a stamp seal with an extended handle.

Shaked Number and Remarks: Shaked 22. The third small object below is indistinct.

Author's Remarks: The *etrog* in shape and style is rather odd. This would hardly be considered an *etrog* by one more familiar with the standardized iconography.

Location: Kadman Numismatic Pavilion of Eretz Israel Museum, Tel Aviv, K-20119.

Bibliography: Arie Kindler, "Lulab and Etrog on a Seal in the Kadman Numismatic Museum," *Museum Haaretz Bulletin* 4, June 1962, p. 34.

8. Seal of Hilkiah Son of Samuel

חלקיא בן שמואל
אמת ושלם
Hilkiah ben Shmuel Emet ve-Shalom
Hilkiah son of Samuel; Truth and Peace
13 × 15 mm
Matrix: Hematite

Description: A *lulab* to right and an *etrog* to left. Inscription round; the letters are so badly spaced that the last letter, the *mēm* of Shalom, is squeezed below the initial consonant of the inscription.

Shaked Number and Remarks: Not in Shaked.

Author's Remarks: This seal, on the presumption it is genuine, is unusual in two respects. The first is the use of the Hebrew *ben* rather than the Aramaic *bar* for the father, something not otherwise seen on these Sasanian seals. The second is the slogan, namely "Truth and Peace." Such phrases appear on Byzantine seals but this is the sole example on a Jewish Sasanian seal that the writer has seen.

The name Hilkiah does not end in an *aleph* in Hebrew, but rather in a *hē*, the name being an abbreviation of חלקיהו, or Hilkiyahu, "Jehovah is my portion." The oddities indicate this is an extraordinarily atypical seal and may be dubious in origin. It clearly resembles, however, Shaked 2, the seal of Juda [. . .] son of Abba.

Location: Collection of Harlan J. Berk, New York, NY.

Bibliography: Christie's Catalogue, "Ancient Jewelry," Auction December 8, 1999, Item 129.

9. Seal of Huna Son of Nathan

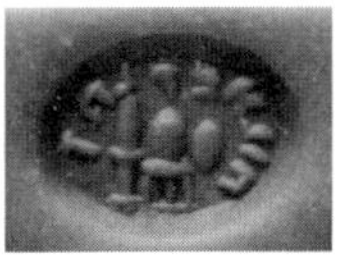

הונא בר נתן
Hunā bar Nathan
11 × 14 mm
Matrix: Faint pink carnelian with white streaks

Provenance: Hecht Collection, University of Haifa.

Description: A *lulab* to left, *etrog* to right, between which is what Shaked describes as probably a small incense shovel, the *maḥtāh* or *yāʿ*, employed in the Temple ritual. Inscription round.

Shaked Number and Remarks: Shaked 9. This is the name of a prominent Jewish leader in fourth-century Sasanian Babylonia. This could well be the seal of the Babylonian exilarch and *amora* of the same name, fourth to the start of the fifth centuries. Thus, it is very important.

Author's Remarks: If the middle object is an incense shovel, as Shaked states, it has a very peculiar handle. It seems more like an ovoid object on a four-legged table. Likewise unusual, the design is on a longer horizontal plane.

Location: Reuben and Edith Hecht Museum, Haifa, H-1934.

Bibliography: Beer (1983), pp. 435ff.; Graetz (1893), vol. 2, 610; and *Encyclopaedia Judaica,* vol. 8, pp. 1075–76.

10. Seal of Samuel

שמואל

Shmuel

12 × 8 mm

Matrix: Garnet

Description: A *lulab* within a rectangular open box to left, an *etrog* to right, and what seems a small animal with bushy tail above to right. Inscription to left.

Shaked Number and Remarks: Shaked 17. Probably because of a poor photograph, Shaked was unsure of the objects depicted.

Author's Remarks: The *lulab* and *etrog* are clear on a good impression. The rodent, looking somewhat like a beaver, is not known from other seals. If a very poorly figured bull, this would indeed be typical on Sasanian seals.

Location: Yale University Babylonian Collection, NCBS 952.

11. Seal of Levi Son of Simon

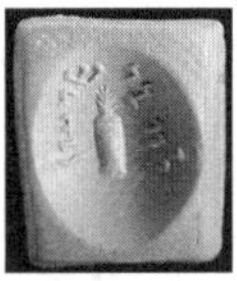

לוי בר שמעון

Levi bar Shimon

13 × 10.5 mm

Matrix: Garnet

Provenance: Former collection of Ahmed Saidi.

Description: In the center a *lulab*. Inscription starts to right and runs across top and then to left.

Shaked Number and Remarks: Not in Shaked.

Author's Remarks: This seal in size and depiction is close in style to Shaked 15, seal of Joseph. The Hebrew letters, though very small, are beautifully cut. The *lulab* rarely appears without the *etrog,* the two major Jewish symbols in Sasanian society. Oddly, though common Jewish names, these have not been observed on other known seals emanating from that cultural milieu.

Location: Private collection.

Bibliography: Not published.

Coin of the Year Three of the Bar Kokhba War
(134/135 C.E.).
Silver tetradrachm, reverse side.
Lulab to right; *etrog* to left.
(For the Freedom of Jerusalem) לחרות ירושלם

SEALS OF ABRAHAM'S BINDING OF ISAAC AND RELATED SCENES (12–26)

12. Seal of Hillel Son of Menasseh

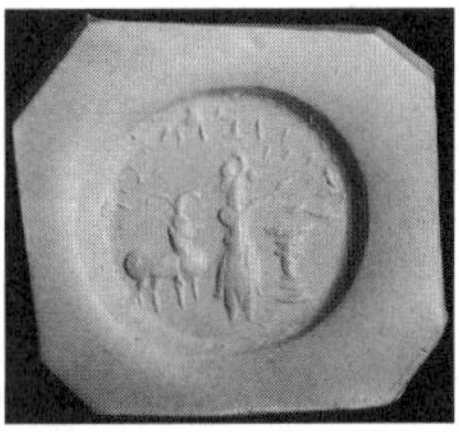

הילל בר מנשה
Hillel bar Menashe
17 mm diam.
Matrix: Hematite
Provenance: Moussa Collection.

Description: The *Aqedah,* Abraham's Binding of Isaac. Abraham in center, frontal, face turned away, left hand extended with knife, before a fire altar, Isaac's body suspended above the altar, and ram to left. Inscription round overhead.

Shaked Number and Remarks: Shaked 16. The patronym is difficult to make out. "Possibly the motif of the sacrifice of Isaac."

Author's Remarks: Edna Engel of the Jewish National and University Library, Hebrew University, kindly put together the scattered parts of the patronym to state that it is Menashe. The image of the *Aqedah* shown is in some respects similar to Christian ones on red earthenware bowls and terra-cotta tiles from North Africa in this same period. Even in the famous Beth-Alpha mosaic, coming from this time, Isaac is likewise suspended in air.

The fire altar, a supreme symbol of the Zoroastrian religion, much like the cross in Christianity, is shown on the reverse of the royal Sasanian coinage, the portrait of the reigning king being on the obverse. Its vaguely similar appearance here may be an indication of cultural assimilation of Jews into the society.

It had been thought by Sasanian sigillographers that The Binding of Isaac portrayal was not used by Jews in the Sasanian Empire, but that theory is disproved by this seal.

Location: Musées royaux d'Art et d'Histoire, Brussels, IR.988.

Bibliography: Lerner (1977), pp. 18–22; Gignoux and Gyselen (1978), pp. 246–47, MCB 16:1, pl. xvii; and *Splendeur des Sassanides: L'empire perse entre Rome et la Chine* [224–642], Musées royaux d'Art et d'Histoire, 1993 (catalogue).

13. Seal of Jacob Son of Judah

יעקב בר יהודה

Yaakov bar Yehuda

15.5 mm diam.

Matrix: Chalcedony

Provenance: Former collection of Ahmed Saidi.

Description: This very unusual seal depicts The Binding of Isaac with an inscription. A bearded Abraham stands facing the altar, holding a knife in his right hand. The body of Isaac, clearly shown, floats slightly over the altar. A ram is to left, tied to a tree between it and Abraham. Over the tree is a hand reaching down, representing the hand of God or his messenger, clearly shown with five fingers as in the Beth Alpha mosaic. In an unusual variant, Abraham's face is turned to the altar rather than toward the hand.

The Hebrew letters of the inscription are above the scene and expertly cut.

Shaked Number and Remarks: Not in Shaked.

Author's Remarks: This seal, including its variant details and expert lettering, tempts one to question its authenticity, particularly because the letters are so crowded together in a small space. Yet the lettering seems not to have been added later because the hand, usually high up, is below the lettering. Of course, the hand may have been added later as well. The combination of the *Aqedah* and a name is extraordinary, as aforementioned.

Location: Private collection.

Bibliography: Not published.

14. Seal Without Inscription: Abraham's Binding of Isaac

20 mm diam.

Matrix: Banded agate

Description: The Binding of Isaac. Abraham with a large cap or helmet,* face turned backward, both hands extended with knife in left hand, before an altar; Isaac's body suspended above the altar. Ram to left, thicket directly behind, a hand extended above thicket. Abraham seems to be looking at the hand, which of course represents the hand of God or his angelic messenger.

Shaked Number and Remarks: Not in Shaked.

Author's Remarks: This seal should be compared to a similar *Aqedah* on Shaked 16, seal of Hillel son of Menasseh, almost exactly the same size but having no thicket or extended hand, and with the body of Isaac being more schematic. This same *Aqedah* is also illustrated in Göbl, 4d: as well as Lerner (1977), pl. IV, No. 24. Reference should likewise be made to Göbl 4c, on the same page as 4d, a line drawing that has the same scene except that there is no body but what seems to be a stick figure floating above the altar and there is no extended hand from above. Located in the British Museum, Department of Western Antiquities (119616), it is a carnelian bezel in a silver ring. The reason for the exclusion of this seal by Shaked, as well as similar ones showing The Binding of Isaac, is that they are more likely Christian.

Location: Bibliothèque Nationale, Paris, No. 1330.

Bibliography: Göbl, p. 37, pl. 2, 4d; Bonner, 344, pl. XIX. Not in Delaporte, vols. 1 and 2.

*Wherever the writer indicates a helmet on these seals, it may well be a turban with straps.

15. Seal Without Inscription: Abraham's Binding of Isaac

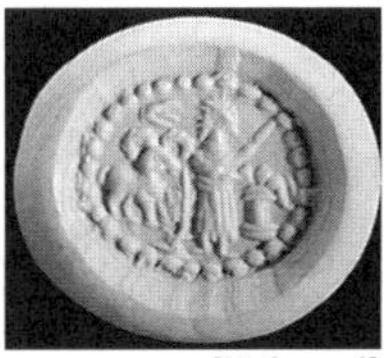

[Enlarged]

11.3 × 12.8 mm

Matrix: Hematite

Description: The Binding of Isaac. Abraham, face turned backward, seems to be looking at a hand extended from on high above the ram, to left, with a bush between Abraham and the ram. Abraham grasps a knife over the altar, which is to right, on which lies the body of Isaac.

Shaked Number and Remarks: Not in Shaked.

Author's Remarks: This seal, though smaller, bears a remarkable resemblance to the Shaked No. 16 aforementioned. Without an inscription it is almost impossible to know whether these types of seals are Jewish or Christian, though most likely they are the latter.

Location: Jonathan P. Rosen Collection.

Bibliography: Not published.

16. Seal Without Inscription: Abraham with Cross on Altar

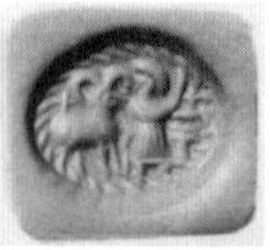

9 × 11 mm

Matrix: Almandine

Description: Abraham stands to right, left hand raising a knife, looking to left toward a ram. To far right there is an altar on which stands a cross. Seal edge encircled by a wreath.

Shaked Number and Remarks: Not in Shaked.

Author's Remarks: Various authors, some distinguished, have raised doubts as to whether these scenes are Jewish or Christian. This seal, where the cross rather than the body of Isaac is shown on the altar, proves, without doubt, the Christian background of certain of these seals.

Location: The British Museum, Department of Western Asiatic Antiquities, London, No. 119837.

Bibliography: Lerner (1977), p. 46. Quoted by Lerner is Bivar, pl. 8: CG3.

17. Seal Without Inscription: Abraham with Cross over Altar

13 × 9 mm

Matrix: Carnelian

Description: Abraham stands to right holding a cross over an altar to left over which floats a stick figure. His head is turned to right in the pose where such seals usually show a ram or the hand from above, but the right edge of the seal is broken off and only a fragmentary image is left.

Shaked Number and Remarks: Not in Shaked.

Author's Remarks: This seal only reinforces the Christian nature of these seals where the sacrifice of Isaac was considered a prefiguration of Christ as seen through the story of Abraham's sacrifice of Isaac.

Location: The British Museum, Department of Western Antiquities, London, No. 119616.

Bibliography: Lerner (1977), pl. V, fig. 31. Quoted by Lerner are Bivar, pl. 5:BD5, and Siegelkanon, 4c.

18. Seal Without Inscription: Abraham with Cross over Altar

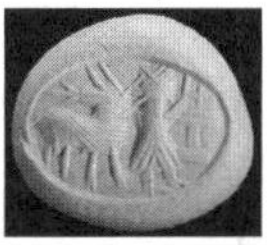

10 × 13 mm

Matrix: Carnelian

Description: A very schematic scene of Abraham, to right, and the ram, to left, with bushes over the ram. To the right of Abraham is an altar, above which appears a cross.

Shaked Number and Remarks: Not in Shaked.

Author's Remarks: This seal is crudely done. The ram's head seems lost in the overhead bushes, presumably thus caught in the thicket. Likewise Abraham's head is indistinct though clearly he is wielding an upright knife over the altar, which, however, has a cross rather than a body. The seal is obviously Christian.

Location: The Wolfe Family Collection, Jerusalem.

Bibliography: Not published.

19. Seal Without Inscription: Abraham Holding Isaac

13.4 × 17 mm

Matrix: Hematite

Description: Abraham stands to left holding a small vertical body. Abraham's head is turned toward a huge ram, larger than he is. There is no altar, bush, thicket, or hand from overhead.

Shaked Number and Remarks: Not in Shaked.

Author's Remarks: This very odd seal can only be identified as Abraham's Binding of Isaac due to certain common features, though without altar or bush of that seal type. Over the hind part of the ram is an object that may be a cross.

Location: Kunsthistorisches Museum, Vienna, No. IX b 1648.

Bibliography: Lerner (1977), pl. V, fig. 34.

20. Seal Without Inscription: Abraham with Crosses

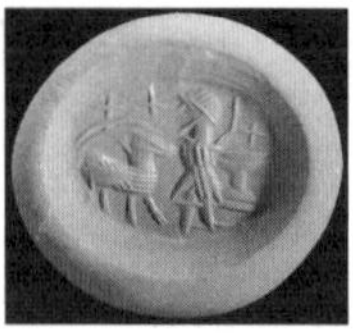

12.7 × 17.4 mm

Matrix: Black, white, and gray banded agate

Description: The *Aqedah.* Abraham, wearing what seems a helmet and with knife in left hand, looks back toward ram. Altar as usual is to right, but instead of Isaac's body, there is a cross. Above the ram are two crosses.

Shaked Number and Remarks: Not in Shaked.

Author's Remarks: This, as has been shown before, is obviously a Christian depiction of The Binding of Isaac.

Location: Jonathan P. Rosen Collection.

Bibliography: Not published.

21. Seal with Latin Inscription: Abraham's Binding of Isaac

19 × 22 mm

Matrix: Nicolo

Inscription: "SERVANDA VIVAS," that is, "By Obedience You Live."

Description: Abraham stands, knife upraised in right hand, holding a bound Isaac with his left hand. A ram stands to left, over which extends from above a hand pointing to Abraham, whose head turns toward the hand. A large fire altar to right is flaming. Abraham is wearing a short cloak, with shoulders and knees exposed. Inscription above.

Shaked Number and Remarks: Not in Shaked.

Author's Remarks: This apparently is not a Sasanian seal but is included to show the common features in the pictorial representation of Abraham's Binding of Isaac among the various religions practiced at that time. The seal is from a Christian area, almost surely late Roman since the Byzantines spoke and wrote mainly in Greek. Oddly, the large flaming fire altar is closer in representation to Zoroastrian practice than the other seals shown with this theme.

Location: Unknown.

Bibliography: "Objects with Semitic Inscriptions, 1100 B.C.–A.D. 700," subtitle, "Jewish, Early Christian and Byzantine Antiquities," Auction XXIII, November 20, 1989, L. Alexander Wolfe and Frank Sternberg, Zurich. No. 353, p. 95. Reference is to Goodenough, vol. III, No. 1041.

22. Seal Without Inscription: Fire Altar and Priest

15 × 18 mm

Matrix: Hematite

Provenance: Former L. P. Cesnola Collection.

Description: A large ram stands to the left of a priest whose turbaned head is turned toward the ram. To the lower right of the priest is a flaming fire altar toward which the priest's arms are extended. Between and above the two figures is a crescent moon.

Shaked Number and Remarks: Not in Shaked.

Author's Remarks: The fire altar is so small in relation to the figures that it is very atypical for a Zoroastrian representation, though the crescent moon would indicate the opposite. Since the seal has no figure on or near the altar, thus eliminating a Christian or Jewish interpretation, it may be possibly as Zoroastrian.

Location: The Metropolitan Museum of Art, Purchase, 1893, No. 93.17.38.

Bibliography: Lerner (1977), p. 54, lists it as 93.22.64; von der Osten, "The Ancient Seals from the Near East," fig. 28.

23. Seal Without Inscription: Abraham's Binding of Isaac(?)

15 mm diam.

Matrix: Hematite

Description: Abraham to right, wearing a helmet with straps, is before an altar to extreme right. His head is turned to left facing a ram. There is nothing on the altar. Above the horns of the ram is a defective area where once perhaps there was a star or moon.

Shaked Number and Remarks: Not in Shaked.

Author's Remarks: Among the many variants of this seal type, it is extraordinary to show such a small empty altar. Yet the iconography is vaguely similar to an *Aqedah* seal.

Location: Ashmolean Museum, Oxford, England, No. 1922; 63.

Bibliography: Lerner (1977), p. 53. Gignoux and Gyselen, 1987, p. 165.

24. Seal Without Inscription: Abraham's Binding of Isaac(?)

20 mm diam.

Matrix: Hematite

Description: Abraham to right, wearing a helmet or cap with straps, stands before a schematic altar to extreme lower right. He holds a knife. There is nothing on the altar. To left stands a large ram, whose horns extend almost to the top of the seal. Nothing else is shown.

Shaked Number and Remarks: Not in Shaked.

Author's Remarks: There is nothing to pinpoint this seal in any known category. The scene is similar to an *Aqedah* representation lacking a body on or near the altar. However, with no hand extending from above, no thicket, and no religious symbols of any type, this seal does not encourage speculation. Perhaps the *Aqedah*-type seals so appealed to a Sasanian, that he ordered this one purely for personal pleasure.

Location: The Louvre, Paris, AO 6136.

Bibliography: Lerner (1977), p. 52 (wrongly sized). Quoted by Lerner in Delaporte, *Louvre* 11, pl. III:25.

25. Seal Without Inscription: Zoroastrian Worship

20 × 18.5 mm

Matrix: Calcified agate

Description: A tall helmeted sentry to left stands on guard facing right before a flaming fire altar, spear held upright in both hands.

Shaked Number and Remarks: Not in Shaked.

Author's Remarks: This is obviously not a Jewish (or Christian) seal but is included because it shows the difference between the treatment of certain seals depicting Zoroastrian religious worship and those showing the *Aqedah*. The sentry shows the *padôm*, a veil cover so his breath will not taint the altar.

Location: Collection of author.

Bibliography: Harlan J. Berk Catalogue Sale of May 20, 2002, lot number 691.

26. Seal Without Inscription: Scene of Worship

19 × 16 mm

Matrix: Chalcedony

Description: A large crowned figure stands to the left of an altar without a knife. Above the altar is an eight-pointed star, higher a crescent moon, and still higher another eight-pointed star. To the left is what seems a palm branch.

Shaked Number and Remarks: Not in Shaked.

Author's Remarks: This almost surely is not the *Aqedah* but probably a scene of Zoroastrian worship at a fire altar, which, however, in superficial iconography is similar. One may speculate that the symbolic convergence of the Zoroastrian representation with the biblical theme may indicate that both flow from what had been a much earlier common tradition.

Location: The British Museum, Department of Western Asiatic Antiquities, London, No. 119382.

Bibliography: E. A. Wallis Budge, *Amulets and Talismans,* New York, 1961, p. 126; Göbl, p. 37, pl. 2. 4b.

Sasanian Coin
Obverse: Bust of Shapur II (309–379 C.E.)
Reverse: Fire altar with elaborate supports.
Dinar. A standard reverse.

SEALS OF THE HUMAN FIGURE (27–29)

27. Seal of Joseph Son of Nata

[Enlarged]

יוסף בר נתא

Yosef bar Nata

12 × 9 mm

Matrix: Banded agate

Description: Standing man to right, bearded, arms outstretched as though in prayer, cords extended to what seem to be bundles above his knees. On both sides are curious figures called half-closed crosses by Shaked. In an unusual form, the inscription starts at lower left and then round at top.

Shaked Number and Remarks: Shaked 7. The dangling bundles (only one according to Shaked) are called girdles. There is a Talmudic scholar named Asi bar Nathan and since Asi is a variant form of Joseph, this might be the same name (cf. Hyman [1964], I:240f.).

Author's Remarks: There are two corded hanging objects but this may only be crude imagery showing the garment and its fluffy bottom. However, it should be noted that the *kustik*, or sacred girdle, was required to be worn by all Zoroastrians. The patronym does not have the final letter *nun* and thus the last name would seem to be Nata and not Natan. On Byzantine and Coptic seals it is common practice to omit letters at the end when the inscriptions are longer than the space available, and it may be true in this culture as well. The standing figure shown is not an uncommon Sasanian representation.

Location: The Israel Museum, 68: 43.42.

Similar Zoroastrian Seal

28. Seal of Isaac Son of Adda

יצחק בר אדה
Yiṣḥaq bar Adda
12 × 10 mm
Matrix: Onyx

Description: Male bust to right with hair gathered to rear in a bun. Inscription round.

Shaked Number and Remarks: Shaked 1. This is the name of a Babylonian sage, cf. Hyman (1964), II:787 (in Hebrew).

Author's Remarks: The Hebrew letters on this seal are clear. Like other such seals, the *ḥēt* and *hē* are very similar.

Location: Staatliche Museum Preussischer Kulturbesitz, Museen für Islamischer Kunst, Berlin, V.A. 1039.

Bibliography: Horn and Steindorff, No. 1039.

Similar Christian Sasanian Seal

29. Seal of Ityonah Yoniya (or Ye'udia)

איתיונה (1) יאניא or (2) יאודיא

17 × 13 mm

Matrix: Orange carnelian

Provenance: Edward Ganz Collection, Department of Near Eastern Studies, University of California, Berkeley.

Description: Male bust to right, bearded with Sasanian-style hairstyle, wings below, and rosette to left. Inscription round.

Shaked Number and Remarks: Shaked 19. The reading is difficult and Shaked suggests אית(ויה) or Itoya for the first word, followed by a question mark, without attempting the second word.

Author's Remarks: The first above reading is what the writer most closely sees, though admittedly several letters are very uncertain. Without the *bar* this may not even be a name but rather a salutary phrase. Shaked also states that 'yty is a Talmudic name and since names in this period were often combined ("Raba" for Rab Abba as an example), the first name might in fact be two names, that is, Ity Yonah (Jonah).

Shalom Sabar of Hebrew University suggests a possible interpretation, the second reading for the last word being a corrupt spelling of Yehuda, which would thus be Ity Yona the Jew. The problem is that without the *hē* this could be a very odd spelling.

The style is early Sasanian. The portrait is standard, appearing on many Sasanian seals, with varying details such as the hairstyle. The wings beneath are often associated with administrative or religious office. Widengren (2002) states that Jews were employed by the government as officials, especially for the purpose of taxation.

Location: Robert H. Lowie Museum, University of California, Berkeley, 109.3.

Similar Zoroastrian Seal

SEALS OF ANIMALS AND OTHER LIFE FORMS (30–41)

30. Seal of Hunay

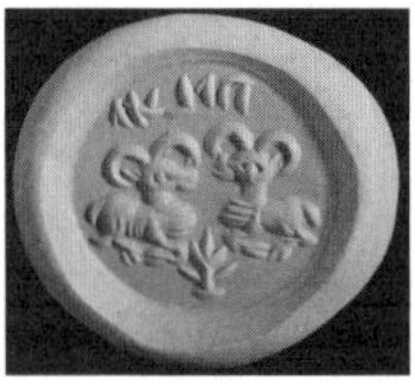

הונאי
Hunay
18 × 19 mm
Matrix: Black, white, and gray banded agate
Provenance: Former collection of Ahmed Saidi.

Description: Two sitting rams facing each other, bushlike object below. Inscription above.

Shaked Number and Remarks: Shaked 18. The reading is somewhat doubtful, and written as described. It might be interpreted as Honi, an early Talmudic figure.

Author's Remarks: The ram had a royal status, and the horns of rams appear on royal crowns and thrones and were objects of royal hunts. The Zodiacal sign Aries (ram) was auspicious; and, significantly, rams were sacrificed at important festivals. The ram is among the more common figures on Sasanian seals for these reasons; its antique origins as a cult object are underscored by the fact that Amon the ram-god was the main deity of Thebes, the ancient Egyptian capital. Coins showing Alexander of Macedon as a divinity depict his head with ram's horns, illustrating the continuity of this symbol.

In Jewish tradition the ram's horn also has great significance, blown on Rosh haShanah because it became associated with the *Aqedah*.

Location: Collection of Jonathan P. Rosen. New York City.

Bibliography: Published by Frank Sternberg AG, 1970. 72,446.

31. Seal Without Inscription: Two Standing Rams

18 × 20.1 mm
Matrix: Seems to be bronze

Description: Two large rams stand facing one another. Abstract designs on each side of rams and above.

Shaked Number and Remarks: Not in Shaked.

Author's Remarks: This is a typical non-Jewish Sasanian seal. The reason for its inclusion is to point out its similarity to the seal of Hunay, thus indicating the high degree of intercultural assimilation in Sasanian society. Bronze seals are quite rare in this culture.

Location: Collection of Jonathan P. Rosen. New York City.
Bibliography: Not published.

32. Seal of Isaac Son of Judah

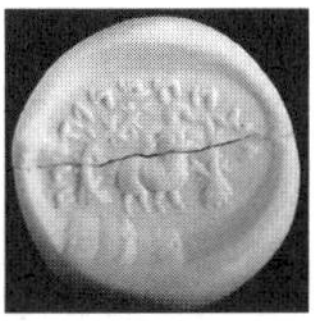

יצחק בר יהודה
Yiṣḥaq bar Yehudah
11.2 × 15.6 mm
Matrix: Discolored white carnelian

Description: Ram on platform between two bushes or trees, the ram butting the one to the right. Inscription round.

Shaked Number and Remarks: Not in Shaked.

Author's Remarks: The cast is unfortunately damaged. The lettering is clear though, as is often the case, the *yōd* and *wāw* can be confused. The seal owner suggests that the ram, which seems tied to the tree on right, could be an abbreviation of The Binding of Isaac. This might be, though without the actual sacrificial altar or figure being shown, as on most other seals of this type, the connection is tentative at best. The ram as a Sasanian royal symbol has been noted.

Location: Jeffrey Spier Collection.
Bibliography: Not published.

33. Seal of Huna Son of Samuel

הונא בר שמואל
Huna bar Shmuel
18 × 13.5 mm
Matrix: Unknown

Provenance: Impression received from unquoted source by Joseph Naveh many years ago.

Description: Bird of prey over a ram. Inscription above.

Shaked Number and Remarks: Shaked 25. This is a poorly photographed seal and the first letters are obscure; the rest seem to be correct. Shaked defines the animal as a gazelle.

Author's Remarks: The writer sees the animal as a ram, often appearing on Sasanian seals. As mentioned before, Huna is a name known from Talmudic history; see, for example, above, No. 9, Huna b. Nathan.

Location: Collection of Joseph Naveh.

34. Seal of Hada Son of Hiyyā

חדא בר חייה

Ḥadā bar Ḥiyyā

16 mm diam.

Matrix: Banded chalcedony

Description: Lion striding to right. Inscription above and to left.

Shaked Number and Remarks: Shaked 6. The Hebrew letters of the first name are unclear, but this is the preferred reading.

Author's Remarks: The writer agrees with Shaked. The third letter of the first name is merely to be guessed at. The lion, with wide jaws, seems to hold something in its mouth but this may be a casting imperfection.

The lion of course is universally regarded in early cultures as reflecting royal status and heroic power. In Zoroastrian society the image is often winged, sometimes with an encircling snake. It would be a logical symbol for Jews, the lion standing for the tribe of Judah as well as the Davidic line, though the lions are usually depicted in pairs.

Location: Staatliche Museen Preussischer Kulterbesitz, Museum für Islamischer Kunst, Berlin, V.A. 1151.

Bibliography: Horn and Steindorff, No. 1151.

Similar Zoroastrian Seal

35. Seal of Jonah

יונה

Jonah

16.0 × 15.7 mm

Matrix: Brown-clear sardonyx

Description: Lion reclining to right, crescent and star below. Inscription a bit to left above. There is some damage to the seal surface at left rear of the lion.

Shaked Number and Remarks: Shaked 12. There is a Palestinian *amora* by this name (cf. Hyman [1964], II:694–97).

Author's Remarks: The name Jonah of course is quite common. Also, Byzantine seal types, which a Palestinian would probably use, are quite different from the Sasanian ones despite the geographical proximity and human traffic flow. Gignoux (see bibliography) tentatively reads the inscription differently. The writer agrees with Shaked though the *yōd* and *wāw* are almost interchangeable here and the third letter is unclear. The combination below the lion of the crescent moon and the star are traditional Jewish symbols whose history goes back to much earlier times.

Location: Cabinet des Médailles, Bibliothèque Nationale, Paris. 1975.7.5.

Bibliography: Gignoux (1978), 4.55; Gyselen (1982), 30.E.54.

Similar Zoroastrian Seal

36. Seal of Ibrami(?)

עברמי

Ibrami (?)

14.8 × 11.6 mm

Matrix: Cream and white banded agate

Description: Frontal face of a lion with thick whiskers. Inscription above.

Shaked Number and Remarks: Not in Shaked.

Author's Remarks: The front-faced lion, sometimes called a lion mask, was common to Roman seals, sometimes within a wreath. It is less common in Sasanian culture, where lions are usually shown in profile walking, sitting, or even sleeping. Examples here are the Jewish seals of Ḥadā son of Ḥiyyā and Jonah.

Though the Hebrew letters are clear, the proper name is less so. עברי of course is Hebrew or Jew. A possible variant, also unclear, may be עברטי (Ibratey).

Location: Collection of Jonathan P. Rosen. New York City.

Bibliography: Not published.

37. Seal of Abba

[Enlarged]

אבא

Abbā

21 mm at widest point. Elongated circle.

Description: Bear walking to right. Inscription above.

Shaked Number and Remarks: Shaked 5. Though the name is common to both Jews and Christians of the period, the Hebrew script proves its owner was Jewish. Göbl (see bibliography) thought it might be Parthian.

Author's Remarks: This mysterious seal is now unloctable. It is not in Bivar; on inquiry, the British Museum wrote that the reference is Pope and Ackerman (1938, pl. 256 HH) was a misattribution.

Location: Unknown

Bibliography: Göbl, p. 44, pl. 16, 45b (first of three).

Similar Zoroastrian Seal

38. Seal of Shem Son of Ḥunar

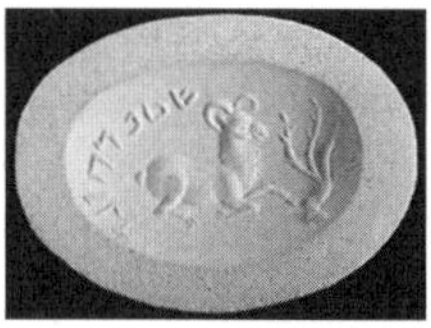
[Enlarged]

שם בר חונר

Shem bar Ḥunar

11 × 15 mm

Matrix: Almandine garnet

Provenance: Henri Seyrig Collection.

Description: Mouflon (wild sheep with horns) reclining to right before bush. Inscription toward left, round.

Shaked Number and Remarks: Shaked 13. The patronym might be חונוי, which would give Shem bar Honi or bar Hunay. In a previous publication (1981), Shaked also questioned the second letter of the first name.

Author's Remarks: The last two letters of the patronym can be read several ways; the writer seems to see a *yōd* at the end, though this may be an imperfection. The mouflon is a common image in Sasanian culture.

Location: Cabinet des Médailles, Bibliothèque Nationale, Paris, 1972–1317, 52.

Bibliography: Gignoux (1978), 8.3. Catalogued as Parthian and read differently. Also Gyselen (1982), 30.L.26.

39. Seal of ᶜUqbā Son of Pāpā

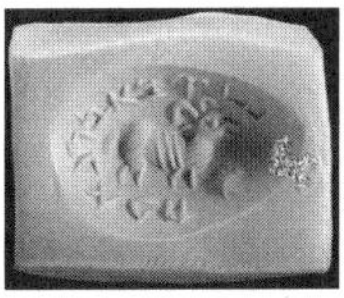

עוקבא בר פאפה
ᶜUqba bar Pāpā
11 × 17 mm
Matrix: Garnet
Provenance: Former Collection of Ahmed Saidi.

Description: Mouflon (wild sheep with horns) standing to right on platform before an object that may be a blossom or small bush. Inscription on top and round to left and below.

Shaked Number and Remarks: Not in Shaked.

Author's Remarks: This seal, in size, material, and subject, is very similar to Shaked 38, also a mouflon; in this case, however, the mouflon is standing rather than reclining. Also Shaked 2 spells the name Papa with an *aleph* at the end rather than a *hē* as here. Variant spellings were not uncommon perhaps because the cutter was not well versed in Hebrew spelling; irregularities were also not considered a problem. Indeed, the cutter may not have been a Jew. This likewise occurs on Jewish medieval seals.

Pāpā, as aforementioned, is a name known from both the Talmud and the Sasanian religious academies, as is ᶜUqba.

Location: Private collection.
Bibliography: Not published.

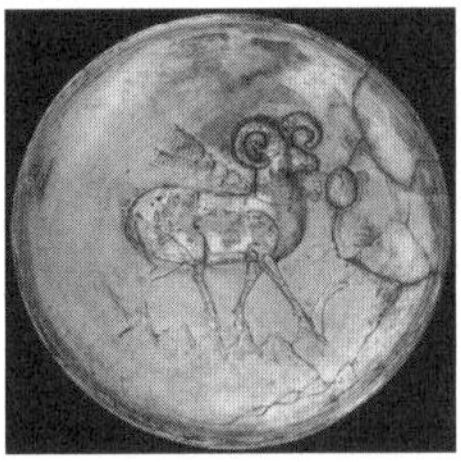

Sasanian plate with mouflon, silver with details Mercury gilded. 21.2 cm in diameter. Museum of Fine Arts, Boston.

40. Seal of Samuel Son of Yosha Tov(?)

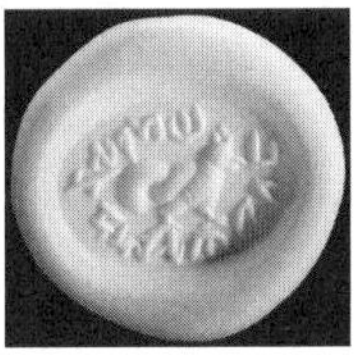

שמואל בר יושעטב
Shmuel bar Yosha Tov
12.6 × 16.4 mm
Matrix: Carnelian
Description: Cock to right, inscription round.
Shaked Number and Remarks: Not in Shaked.

Author's Remarks: This cock has a full bushy tail, not seen elsewhere, but no other bird fits the depiction. The cock is rarely shown on Sasanian seals. It is a beneficent symbol, arousing mankind at dawn to good deeds, and thus, with the light, a worker against demons and sorcerers. The cock is also an ancient motif in Judaism and appears on the seal of Yeho'ahaz, son of the king from the seventh century B.C.E. (Avigad, *Corpus,* No. 13), which is to say over a thousand years earlier; and is shown as well on Greek coins from the earliest period of coinage, ca. 500 B.C.E. The cock likewise is featured on Jewish seals from the late medieval period.

The last part of the inscription is difficult. Spier translates the last word as "Good" though Tov is also a proper name. The next-to-last letter, however, is unclear.

Location: Jeffrey Spier Collection.

Bibliography: Not published.

41. Seal of Vashish(?)

[Enlarged]

ח וששׁ

7.8 × 9.2 mm

Matrix: Carnelian

Description: Pheasant to right, inscription to upper left, floating Hebrew letter lower right.

Shaked Number and Remarks: Not in Shaked.

Author's Remarks: The first two letters of the description are clear, the third letter seeming to be a *shin* with, however, an odd horizontal line crossing toward the top of the last vertical line of the letter. Separate from the inscription, below to right, is a letter, possibly a *ḥēṯ,* standing for "Life." The problem here, as elsewhere, is that there are variant letter forms from this period. The horizontal line may indicate a contraction, referring to another letter. The name, if it be a name, is not otherwise attested.

The pheasant and the peacock were prized in Sasanian culture for both their beauty and their rich taste. There are many seals from this culture depicting the pheasant; it also appears on silverware and textiles.

Location: Collection of Jonathan P. Rosen. New York City.

Bibliography: Not published.

SEALS OF FAMILY DEVICES (42–43)

42. Seal of Abba Son of Malka(?)

אבה בר מהלכא
Abba bar Malka(?)
17.8 mm diam.
Matrix: Sardonyx
Provenance: Ex-Collection Pirouzan, Teheran.

Description: Eight-ray star over crescent moon, scorpion below. Inscription round.

Shaked Number and Remarks: Shaked 11. The star might stand for the sun, as it can in this combination. Shaked feels this is the correct interpretation. A different series of readings are possible for the patronym, Shaked suggesting five possibilities of which he tentatively prefers מחויא.

Author's Remarks: The letters are sloppy, the *hē* and *ḥēṯ*, as has been stated before, often being indistinguishable on these Sasanian seals. Although the second consonant of the father's name is not otherwise met with in the Aramaic *Malka*, the writer feels this is the closest reading possible. A Talmudic writer states that the scorpion is a symbol of the Jewish people.

Location: Bibliothèque Nationale, Paris, 1970.327.

Bibliography: Gignoux (1978), 8.7. Catalogued as Parthian and read differently. Also Gyselen (1982), 50.B.5.

Similar Zoroastrian Seal

Sasanian stucco plaque from Um-Za'atir near Ctesiphon. Metropolitan Museum, New York.

43. Seal of Aḥa Son of Sumāqā

אחא בר סומקא

Aḥa bar Sumāqā

17.7 × 15.7 mm

Matrix: Lapis lazuli

Provenance: Ex-Collection Dieulafoy.

Description: Device with crescent moon above surmounted by what resembles the number 7. Inscription round, followed by three large dots.

Shaked Number and Remarks: Shaked 4. In an earlier publication (1977, p. 24) Shaked transcribed the name as above, but changed his mind (1981) and thought the first name was Rūḥā; initially he had stated that the patronym is reminiscent of the Talmudic name Abbā Simmuqyad.

Author's Remarks: This writer agrees with the original 1977 reading where the patronymic refers to the sumac, or red dye, trade. Sasanian personal or clan devices were common; these somewhat arbitrary abstract insignias often in the later period absorbed elements of monograms. They were highly prized and resulted in many duplicates when used by members of the same family or clan. Literary sources indicate that they functioned somewhat like the seals themselves as marks of identification.

Location: The Louvre, Paris, A.O.D. 168. Now deposited at the Cabinet des Médailles, Bibliothèque Nationale, Paris.

Bibliography: Delaporte I, D. 278, p. 84, pl. 56, fig. 53. (Likewise catalogued as Aḥa, not Rūḥā.) Also Gignoux (1978), 8.8, and Gyselen (1982), 70.68.

Similar Zoroastrian Seal

MISCELLANEOUS AND DUBIOUS SEALS (44–48)

44. Seal of John

[Enlarged]

(First Line) קבילה Qabīla
(Second Line) יוחנן Yoḥanan
16 mm diam.

Matrix: Brown and white agate

Provenance: Mohsen Foroughi Collection.

Description: Two lines. No depiction.

Shaked Number and Remarks: Shaked 8. The last letter of the first word is smudged and might be a *tāv* rather than a *hē*. The interpretation of the first word is difficult, possibly "I received" in Aramaic written in Hebrew letters.

Author's Remarks: The writer, for lack of a better interpretation, accepts the Shaked preferred reading, though the second line seems garbled. This interesting seal may be a receipt acknowledgment of goods by a buyer named John. As mentioned in the preceding text, according to a tentative analysis of Frye (1968, p. 118), certain Sasanian seals can be classified by function: the largest ones belonging to the officials who certified goods; those of medium size owned by the persons involved in the transaction; while the smaller ones could be those of witnesses. The small seals discussed thus may all be signet ring stones, while this seal might fit the medium-size type.

Bibliography: Frye (1971), p. 9.

45. Seal of Yoash the Dayyan Son of Judah(?)

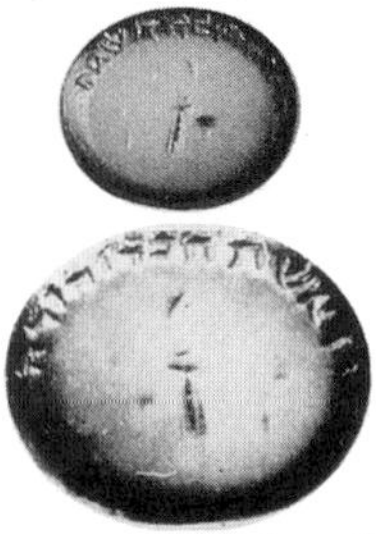
[Enlarged]

יאש ה[דן] בר יהודה
Yo'ash haDin bar Yehuda(?)
13 × 15.5 mm

Matrix: Gemstone, nicolo

Description: "Motif erased. Around the shoulder, inscription."

Shaked Number and Remarks: Shaked 14. The inscription is written at top over what seems to be one previously erased. In the center there is an object, over one also erased, which may have been a fire altar. The inscription itself is subject to several interpretations.

Author's Remarks: This writer has only seen the photograph. There is a hodgepodge of Hebrew letters crudely cut into the stone above the semi-effaced image. The seal, judging by photographic evidence, may be inauthentic.

Bibliography: *Objects with Semitic Inscriptions: 1100 B.C.–A.D. 700,* Auction XXIII, Nov. 20, 1989, L. Alexander Wolfe and Frank Sternberg, "Sassanian Hebrew," p. 31, No. 47.

46. Seal of Isaac Son of Moses

[Enlarged]

יצחק בן משה

Yitzḥak ben Moshe

10 × 18 mm at widest point. Elongated hexagon.

Matrix: Not known

Description: Two-line inscription with a star at the end of the first line.

Shaked Number and Remarks: Shaked 3. The only representation is a drawing as listed below in the bibliography. No location is given.

Author's Remarks: Mordtmann (see bibliography) simply states, "Gem with a Hebrew legend." The line drawing, as illustrated, either is a fake or a curiosa that is not Sasanian. The use of *ben* for father, rather than *bar*, is with one possible exception not seen on any known authentic Sasanian Jewish seal. The shape is wrong for the same reason. The lettering is most peculiar and the last two letters of the patronym seem gibberish.

Bibliography: Mordtmann, IX, p. 51, pl. VI.

47. Seal of Yosine Arcohen [Chief Priest] Son of Iyf … Shalom

(obverse) יוס [ינא אר] כון

(reverse) בן איפ [...] שלוס

13.5 mm

Matrix: Lead

Provenance: Anton Tskalec Collection, Vienna.

Description: Two-sided. Eight-pointed stars in center, inscriptions round. Pearled edges.

Shaked Number and Remarks: Shaked 24. Said to come from southern Lebanon and datable to the seventh century C.E., "Lead bulla, with a design imprinted on both sides. Published in Dexinger and Seibt 1981: 304 ff." The readings are doubtful.

Author's Remarks: Werner Seibt kindly sent the writer the article referred to, with the title "A Hebrew Lead Seal from the Period of the Sasanian Occupation of Palestine (614–629 A.D.)." Seibt, who is one of the leading scholars of Byzantine seals, does not categorically state this is a Sasanian seal but rather that it might come from the very brief period when the Sasanians occupied Palestine and thus be influenced by that reason. In fact, he specifically remarks that two points refer to the Byzantine area: that lead was used as the matrix; and that it is a double-sided seal. He sums up this point conclusively, "In the Sasanian Empire, the eastern neighbor of Byzantium, one-sided seals were used."

In the opinion of the writer, by every measure, double-sided imprint, material, and area where found, this should be considered a Byzantine Jewish seal whether made under Byzantium or the neo-Persians.

This seal is not illustrated.

Bibliography: As above stated.

48. Seal of Samuel Son of Isaac Rabba (or Rava)

[Enlarged]

(first line) שמו אל בן

(second line) Arabic script

(third line) יצחׄ רבה

16 × 10 mm

Matrix: Flat red stone, possibly garnet

Description: Rectangle. Three lines, the first and third being Hebrew script, the second line Arabic script. The third line concludes with a star. No depiction.

Shaked Number and Remarks: Not in Shaked, though mentioned in an earlier work (1977, p. 26).

Author's Remarks: The writer is indebted to Shalom Sabar of Hebrew University, who pointed out that the first word of the third line may be a contraction, the missing last letter, which should be a *kof*, possibly being indicated by a top mark after the previous letter.

The writer is also indebted to Luke Treadwell of Oxford University, who translated the Arabic of the second line as a name, that is, Abī ʿAlī Ibn Ja-ahd (or Ja-ahdh). Presumably the two men mentioned on the seal, one Jewish and the other Muslim, were partners and the seal might have been for commercial use. The name in Arabic indicates the seal is almost surely post-Sasanian, as does the use of *ben* rather than *bar*, but it is included for its interesting background.

Location: Mohsen Foroughi Collection, as of 1971.

Bibliography: Frye (1971), p. 18, pl. XXXII.

FANTASY SEALS ON THE THEME OF THE BINDING OF ISAAC (49-51)

49. Fantasy Seal on the Theme of the Binding of Isaac

27.5 mm diam., with clipped corners

Matrix: Green agate

Provenance: Former collection of Michael Ehrenthal, New York City.

Description: In the center a bearded Abraham stands to right, a long knife in left hand ready to plunge down into an erect Isaac, who is kneeling above a stool before a small flaming fire altar to right. Above the altar a winged angel hovers, left hand pointing to Isaac, right hand suspended over the knife in a warning gesture. To the left of Abraham is a ram; still more to the left, a towering bush in the form of a palm frond, leaning over Abraham's head, almost reaching on high a crescent moon.

Shaked Number and Remarks: Not in Shaked.

Author's Remarks: This delightful and exquisite seal is a large fantasy on the *Aqedah*. In no way could it be Sasanian; it has such full detail on the biblical story one might even call it a parody despite the marvelous workmanship.

According to the records, it came from Persia and possibly derives from the fifteenth or sixteenth century. Its origin, in the opinion of the writer, is far more recent.

Location: Private Collection, New York City.

Bibliography: Not published.

50. A Second Fantasy Seal on the *Aqedah* Theme

19 × 29 mm, oval

Matrix: Sardonyx

Provenance: Former Collection of Michael Ehrenthal, New York City.

Description: This seal is very much like the seal before described, though oval. There are, however, small differences. Isaac kneels above a small table rather than a stool. To bottom right what would seem to be an altar has resting on it a crescent moon, with another crescent moon over the menacing knife of Abraham, while a six-pointed star appears over the ram.

Shaked Number and Remarks: Not in Shaked.

Author's Remarks: This beautifully carved seal, probably coming from the same workshop as the previous 27.5 mm seal—and hence modern in issue rather than Sasanian—is a fantasy on the *Aqedah*, produced possibly from a Muslim workshop due to the odd placing of the crescent moon on the altar, as well as the star above the ram.

The crescent moon over the left knife is described in a sale description allegorically as "The hand of God," but this is completely illogical since the angel stopping the knife is fully shown; thus, the hand would be redundant.

Location: Private Collection, New York City.

Bibliography: Not published.

51. A Third Fantasy Seal on the *Aqedah* Theme

23 × 21

Matrix: Carnelian

Provenance: Former Collection of Michael Ehrenthal, New York City.

Description: Abraham in center, with his right hand being caught by an angel flying to left. He is dressed in a flowing gown, with the top part wallowing in the breeze, a figure straight out of *The Arabian Nights*. His left hand rests on Isaac, who stands upright on a pile of twigs over the altar. To the extreme right grows a vine. To the left is a bush in which is entrapped a small ram. The seal edge is encircled by a plant design. The matrix is part of a complete ring carved out of carnelian.

Shaked Number and Remarks: Not in Shaked.

Author's Remarks: One has to wonder about the gullible nature of collectors to believe they could think such an obviously fraudulent piece would be cut before the twentieth century. It may be, however, that the seal was bought for its obvious beauty, which is a legitimate reason.

Location: Private Collection, New York City.

Bibliography: Not published.

SEALS OF DANIEL IN THE LIONS' DEN (52–57)

52. Seal Showing Daniel in the Lions' Den

[Enlarged]

12 mm diam.

Matrix: Almandine

Description: Daniel stands between two lions, head to right, both hands raised. The ill-formed lions, apart from Daniel, are in a frumpy way rampant but seem the reverse of ferocious, each turning their heads away from Daniel. A band surrounds the seal; the photo seems to be taken from the matrix rather than a cast.

Shaked Number and Remarks: Not in Shaked.

Author's Remarks: The lions in this seal seem more like fluffy chicks. Without a general knowledge of the iconography of similar seals, one would never think this was Daniel in the Lions' Den, but the general position of the figure plus the two animals must lead to the belief the seal is of the genre. No crosses are shown. As Shalom Sabar has pointed out to this writer, Daniel in an orante position in this period was extremely popular in portrayals in Christian catacombs, sarcophagi, and the like.

Location: The British Museum, Department of Western Asiatic Antiquities, No. 119821.

Bibliography: Lerner (1977), pl. VI, fig. 38. Quoted by Lerner are Smirnov, fig. 12; Segal, pl. IV:b; Bivar, pl. 8:CG8; and *Siegelkanon*, 2d.

53. Seal Showing Daniel in the Lions' Den

[Enlarged]

11 × 9 mm

Matrix: Almandine

Provenance: Former C. W. King Collection.

Description: A turbaned male figure to right in a long robe stands with hands crooked above two poorly depicted lions that Lerner claims to have their heads down. There are no crosses.

Shaked Number and Remarks: Not in Shaked.

Author's Remarks: The two lions are so crudely done they seem to be miniatures, but they do not seem upside down. Behind the lion to left is a ribbon-like object with no clear meaning unless it is a long tail. If it were not for the clear iconographic relation to other seals, which without doubt represent Daniel in the Lions' Den, this seal would not be included. The feeling is Christian for this same reason.

Location: The Metropolitan Museum of Art, 1881, No. 81.6.276.

Bibliography: Lerner (1977), p. 59; von der Osten, "The Ancient Seals from the Near East," fig. 107.

54. Seal Showing Daniel in the Lions' Den

13 × 14.5 mm

Matrix Lapis lazuli

Description: Daniel to right, wearing what seems to be a turban, upraised long knives or swords in each hand, is flanked on each side—though not touching them—by two rampant lions, the one to the left poorly depicted.

Shaked Number and Remarks: Not in Shaked.

Author's Remarks: Though other interpretations of this scene have been made, it seems indisputable that this is the biblical representation of Daniel. A favorite iconographic subject of Christians, less so of Jews in this period, if at all, it may safely be assumed to be Daniel in the Lions' Den. There are, however, no crosses shown.

Location: The Wolfe Family Collection, Jerusalem.

Bibliography: Not published.

55. Seal Showing Daniel in the Lions' Den

[Enlarged]

12.5 mm diam.

Matrix: Carnelian

Description: Daniel to right, wearing what seems to be a helmet, holding in his right hand what could be a long knife, stands between two objects, presumably lions—though very crudely depicted—with heads shown as loops above horizontal coils. Above the presumed lions are small horizontal lines, definitely not crosses.

Shaked Number and Remarks: Not in Shaked.

Author's Remarks: If it were not for the common iconography of this seal type, one would neither define the two vertical objects flanking the central figure as lions nor the figure itself as Daniel. One possible explanation for the coils beneath the so-called heads of these rampant objects might be Daniel 6:22, "My God hath sent his angel, and hath shut the lions' mouths, that they have not hurt me."

Location: University of Pennsylvania Museum, Philadelphia, B9403, where the seal is described as "Persian Hero, 2 lions."

Bibliography: Lerner (1977), p. 64, written as CB5 9403. Lerner refers to Legrain, pl. XXXV:738.

56. Seal Showing Daniel in The Lions' Den

12 mm diam.

Matrix: Amethyst

Provenance: Former Greville J. Chester Collection.

Description: Daniel stands legs together, feet contrary, arms stretched horizontally, head to left. Beneath each arm, but not touching Daniel, is a sitting lion, facing outward. Above both of Daniel's arms is a cross. The seal is encircled by a wreath. The photo is taken from the seal matrix and not a cast.

Shaked Number and Remarks: Not in Shaked.

Author's Remarks: This seal, with a cross over each of Daniel's arms, is another bit of incontrovertible evidence that points to the Christian interpretation of the biblical story. The only oddity is the sitting (not rampant or crouching) position of the lions, but it would seem this was because of the designer's lack of space due to the outstretched arms of Daniel with enough space needed above them to put in the crosses.

Location: Ashmolean Museum, Oxford, England, No. 1968; 1217.

Bibliography: Lerner (1977), p. 60. Quoted by Lerner is C. D. E. Fortnum, *The Archaeological Journal*, XXXVII (1880), p. 362, No. 11; Gigoux and Gyselen, 1987, p. 164.

57. Seal Showing Daniel in The Lions' Den

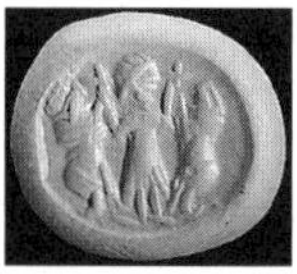

12.5 × 14 mm

Matrix: Carnelian

Description: Daniel wearing what seems to be a helmet stands to right, but rather than long knives or swords he raises a cross in each hand. He is flanked by two rampant lions, which he does not touch. The crosses held in each hand clearly indicate that this is a Christian seal. Judith A. Lerner's study of this subject, *Christian Seals of the Sasanian Period,* proves without doubt the figure shown on these seals is not Herakles or some earlier mythical subject.

Location: The Wolfe Family Collection, Jerusalem.

Bibliography: Not published.

Daniel in the Lions' Den
Christian seal showing cross ca. sixth century C.E.
Images of Inspiration, J. G. Weitenholz, ed.
No. 31, p. 61. Jerusalem, 2000

7 Specific Character of the Known Sasanian Jewish Seals

1. The male bust facing right, bearded, a typical Sasanian pose, is shown on the seals of Joseph son of Nata, Isaac son of Adda, and Ityonah Yoniya (or Ye'udia) (Nos. 27, 28, and 29).

2. The hair is often shown in twisted curl locks, as is that of Ityonah (No. 29). On the basis of cursive inscriptions, this hairstyle is indicative of the late Sasanian period. There is some evidence that Ityonah was an official because of the similarity to such seals from Qasr-i Abu Nasr. This is reinforced by the wing design beneath his bust.

3. Quite common on seals from this period are standing figures with hands outstretched in a gesture of reverence or offering, as shown on the seal of Joseph son of Nata (No. 27). This resembles a reverential figure on the reverse of a Byzantine Jewish bulla roughly from the same time where, however, the worshipper is on bended knees with hands cast down.

4. Lions shown on Sasanian seals are most often striding or recumbent, of which we have an example of each type in the seals of Ḥadā son of Ḥiyyā and Jonah (Nos. 34 and 35). The head of the lion is often turned full front with a *T*-shaped brow and nose and two dot eyes—a style directly derived from the much earlier Babylonian cylinder seals—as also on the seal of Jonah. When

striding, as in the seal of Ḥadā, the lion's tail curves down and then up behind the body.

Though lions on larger seals were shown on those of priests, individuals of lesser importance, as in the above two examples, were not forbidden to use a lion motif.

5. The *kustik*, or sacred girdle, was required to be worn by all Zoroastrians. Perhaps this is the unclear dangling object shown on the seal of Joseph son of Nata (No. 27), which surely indicates great cultural assimilation.

6. Note the somewhat close resemblance of the altar on which Isaac is being sacrificed in the seal of Hillel bar Menashe (No. 12) to the fire altar shown on seals of Zoroastrian worship. The Christian example shown of the same scene (No. 17) is even closer in style.

7. The monogram of Aḥa son of Sumāqā (No. 43) is typical of the monograms shown on the seals of high Sasanian officials and could thus indicate Aḥa was an important person.

8. The moufflons on the seals of Shem son of Ḥunar and ʿUqbā son of Pāpā (Nos. 38 and 39) are one of the more common figures on Sasanian seals as well as on decorative objects. Their meaning has been previously discussed.

9. The *lulab/etrog* combination is the only specific Jewish feature not appearing on non-Jewish Sasanian seals. Seals such as No. 9, that of Hunā son of Nathan (which probably belonged to the well-known exilarch and *amora* of that name), seem to be empirical evidence that the men who used these symbols on their seals were high religious figures. An example of this combination without a name on one seal may likewise indicate—as in non-Jewish Sasanian seals of high officials—that an office rather than a specific individual was referred to. The very large number of these seals, relatively speaking, may indicate they were preserved out of reverence for the highly placed individuals, unlike those of merchants or witnesses, which were thrown away after death.

Notes

CHAPTER 1

1. Frye (1973) claims that the Sasanian period ran from ca. 224 to 651. The terminal date of 642 is also used. Neusner states 226–651.

2. Jerome (ca. 340–420), the great Christian scholar and saint, lived thirty-four years in Bethlehem and was fluent in Hebrew. He wrote that in his time there hardly remained a tenth part of Palestinian Jewry compared to the earlier period. By the start of the seventh century, the Jews were a minority of only 10 to 15 percent of the population of Palestine according to Neusner (1986), p. 245.

3. "The artistic style displays Mesopotamian frontality and the figures wear Iranian dress." Grant (1984), p. 275.

4. "In Babylonia there was a strong tradition that the famous synagogue Shaf Ve-Yativ in Nehardea had been established by the Exiles of Jehoiachin." *Encyclopaedia Judaica*, vol. 15, col. 580. This is not generally accepted by modern scholarship.

5. Baron (1952), p. 211. The reference does not supply details.

6. Gabbay (2002), p. 21. As to the Prophet Daniel—the subject of the twenty-second book of the Hebrew Bible—rabbinical sources maintained he died in Israel (*Midrash Rabba*, commentary on Song of Songs 5:5; Babylonian Talmud, "Sanhedrin," 93b). According to Iranian tradition—devoid of any historical or archaeological evidence—a domed shrine in Shūsh (Susa), a city near the border of Iraq north of the Persian Gulf, holds Daniel's tomb. The crypt beneath the domed chamber houses a grave with no inscription.

7. Neusner (1970), pp. 30–31. Zvi Avneri states, however, that there was some persecution at the start of Ardashir's reign. *Encyclopaedia Judaica*, vol. 4, col. 40. In Neusner's

later work, *Israel and Iran in Talmudic Times* (1986), he is a bit more in accord with Avneri. See "V. Ardashir and the Jews," starting on p. 17. At worst, however, the persecutions could not be compared to those that occurred in later Christian Europe.

8. Widengren (1961), pp. 119, 139. See also Widengren (2002), pp. 36–38.

9. There were however still intermarriage and embrace of Judaism. The famous Babylonian *amora* Mari ben Issur (the Proselyte) had that name because his father was born a non-Jew.

10. Baron (1952), pp. 178–79. Jews also served in high positions in the Sasanian armies, elevated to "even that of a *marzbān* and commander of an army under whom many thousand horsemen served." Widengren (2002), p. 39.

11. Baron (1952), 205. As per the commandment in Deuteronomy 11:20.

CHAPTER 2

1. Graetz (1893), p. 548.

2. The Mongolian invasion and violent destruction in the thirteenth century, especially in the eastern part of what had been the Sasanian Empire, may be a factor in this matter.

CHAPTER 3

1. Malka was an early god shown on a fifth-century Near Eastern representation. Malka (queen) was also the name of a river in Babylonia. The canal on the shore of the Euphrates where it meets the Tigris in southern Mesopotamia was called the Nahar (or Nahr) Malka, that is, the Royal Canal. Malka was likewise the name of the two late *geonim*, Malka b. Aḥa (771) at Pumbedita; and Malka (885) at Sura. It thus seems apparent that places gave their names to Babylonian Jews, which occurred as well in Europe.

2. Neusner (1970), p. 146. See also Neusner's later work, *Israel and Iran in Talmudic Times* (1986), for a review of these complicated events (pp. 218–27, 232–34). The material in many cases is confusing and even contradictory in the writings of respected scholars.

3. It is as though some ancient text in the very far future would refer to what had been a transit center named JFK, and a contemporary would wonder what that stood for.

CHAPTER 4

1. A contemporary fourth- or fifth-century North African plate, Christian in origin, shows The Binding of Isaac with a lion, ram, and bear on its circling edge. As to the scorpion, it has ancient roots. Represented still earlier in Babylonia, scorpions were regarded as religious symbols starting in the late Kassite period (Middle Babylonian, 1651–1157 B.C.E.). There the scorpion is labeled a symbol of the goddess Ishara, equated with Ishtar. Because of its painful sting it was considered an image of power and protection, with tail raised in threat. It thus entered as the constellation Scorpio in the Zodiac. Though also viewed as a demon-created vermin in the Zoroastrian religion, it was likewise on Sasanian seals considered, in a throwback to earlier centuries, as a symbol of good-fortune protection.

2. Bivar (1969), pp. 27–29.

3. Arie Kindler, former director of the Kadman Numismatic Museum in Tel Aviv, now the Eretz-Israel Museum, in personal correspondence stated that the *lulab/etrog* combination on Sasanian seals suggested it was the initial national emblem of the Jews, encountered first on the Judean quarter and half shekels of the fourth year of the First Jewish War and then on the tetradrachms of each of the three years of the later Bar Kokhba War. Though the seven-branched menorah does appear on a small bronze coin of the Maccabean leader Mattathias (Mattatayah) Antigonus (40–37 B.C.E.), it only became a prominent Jewish symbol in the third century C.E., often accompanied by a *lulab* and *etrog*. It is thus Dr. Kindler's opinion, shared by this author, that the *lulab/etrog* combination was a conservative retention of the old symbols, never superseded by the menorah in the earlier-formed Babylonian Diaspora. The rarity of Old Testament themes on those seals also suggests that Jewish national symbols began to be preferred, of which of course the *lulab*, *etrog*, and shofar are prime examples.

4. Younger (1988), p. xi.

5. Frye (1968), pp. 118–32. See also Frye (1970), pp. 79 and 80, where he observes that there are usually one large "official" seal impression, one large "personal" seal impression, and one to ten impressions of small seals, those of the "witnesses." Gropp (1974), pp. 124 and 125, suggests that both large seals might belong to the dignitary sealing the document, one being his seal as functionary of the king, the land, or the magi administration, the other being his personal seal of identity and name.

6. Upton, in Frye (1973), p. 23.

7. Unvala (1953), pp. 55–57.

8. Ackerman, in Pope and Ackerman (1938–39), pp. 785–87.

9. Göbl (1973), pp. 14–16.

10. Brunner (1978), p. 9.

11. See Frye (1973).

12. Herzfeld (1935), p. 107.

CHAPTER 5

1. The confusion on this point is inexplicable to one knowing the form of Yasna, the Zoroastrian worship. The liturgy was conducted inside the precincts of a fire temple. Within an enclosure the silver-metal fire vase was set upon a stone stand, the head priest sitting or standing during the ceremony on a stone seat. Two priests wearing turbans and white masks conducted the liturgy. Obviously, there is no relation between these seal images and this ceremony, though the reverses of the royal Sasanian currency do show a very abbreviated ceremony that has some similarity to the seals considered to represent the Binding of Isaac. See Williams and Boyd (1993), pp. 26–28.

2. Lerner (1977), pp. 36–39, Nos. 31–55.

3. Shaked (1977), p. 18.

4. On Sasanian Jewish magic bowls of this same period, despite Jewish belief in one God, references were often made to deities of other religions, past and present, in order to enhance the protective power. Neusner (1986) specifically states, "magic bowls were used in common by Christians, Mazdeans [Zoroastrians], Jews, and Mandeans, and,

as we have noted, considerable credence was placed by both Jews and pagans in one another's traditions on astrology, medicine, and magic" (pp. 64–65).

5. Gyselen (1998), p. 44.

6. Bezalel Narkiss in Weitzman (1979) points out that no biblical scenes appear in Jewish art between the sixth and thirteenth centuries, possibly due to a combination of the rise of Islam, which forbade human representation in religious art, and Byzantine iconoclasm. Most of these seals are considered to have been made in the middle to the latter period of Sasanian rule, fourth to sixth centuries.

Lee I. Levine (1999) states in his discussion of the ancient synagogue, "although far less frequently displayed than the above-noted symbols (i.e., the Torah ark, menorah, shofar, *lulab* and *etrog*), are biblical scenes. Only a handful is known from ancient Palestine: David at Gaza and possibly also at Meroth, Daniel at Na'aran and Susiya, the '*Aqueda* (binding of Isaac) at Bet Alpha, and a rediscovered '*Aqueda* scene at Sepphoris together with a scene of Abraham and the three angels (Genesis XIX). Diaspora synagogues, too, are markedly reticent in this regard, having but a few biblical depictions. The major exception to this generally sparse picture is the stunning synagogue of Dura Europos in Syria, so exceptional as to defy explanation" (p. 157).

7. These images appear as Christian on gold glasses, terra-cotta plates, gems, seals, textiles, and catacomb wall paintings, and in quite a few cases are conjoined with images from the New Testament.

8. Lerner (1977), p. 28.

Bibliography

Baron, Salo W. *A Social and Religious History of the Jews*, II, Part II. Philadelphia, 1952.

Bivar, A. D. H. *Catalogue of Western Asiatic Seals in the British Museum. Stamp Seals. II: The Sasanian Dynasty*. London, 1969.

Black, Jeremy, and Anthony Green. *Gods, Demons and Symbols of Ancient Mesopotamia: An Illustrated Dictionary*. Austin, Tex., 1992.

Bonner, Campbell. *Studies in Magical Amulets, Chiefly Graeco-Egyptian*. University of Michigan Studies. Numismatic Series 49. Ann Arbor, 1950.

Brunner, Christopher J. *Sasanian Stamp Seals in the Metropolitan Museum of Art*. New York, 1978.

Budge, E. A. Wallis. *Amulets and Talismans*. New Hyde Park, 1961.

Clanchy, M. T. *From Memory to Written Record: England 1066–1307*. Oxford, 1993.

Delaporte, Louis. *Catalogue des cylindres, cachets et pierres gravées de style oriental. Musée du Louvre*. 2 vols. Paris, 1920–23.

Dexinger, Ferdinand, and Werner Seibt. "A Hebrew Lead Seal from the Period of the Sasanian Occupation of Palestine (614–629 A.D.)," pp. 303–17, in *Revue des études Juives* 140. Paris, 1981.

Encyclopaedia Judaica. Vols. 2, 4, 8, 11, and 14. Jerusalem, 1972.

Frye, Richard N. "Sasanian Clay Sealings in the Collection of Mohsen Foroughi," pp. 118–32, in *Iranica Antiqua VIII*. London, 1968.

______. "Sasanian Seal Inscriptions," pp. 79, 80, in *Beiträge zur alten Geschichte and deren Nachleben. Festschrift für Franz Altheim zum 6.10.68.* (Berlin, 1970), Vol. 2, pp. 79, 80.

______ . *Sasanian Seals in the Collection of Mohsen Foroughi*. Corpus Inscriptionum Iranicarum. Part III, Pahlavi Inscriptions. Vol. VI: Seals and Coins. London, 1971.

______. *Sasanian Remains from Qasr-i Abu Nasr, Seals, Sealing and Coins*. Cambridge, Mass., 1973.

Gabbay, Elias Yassi. "Esther's Tomb," in *Esther's Children: A Portrait of Iranian Jews*. Philadelphia, 2002.

Ghirsham, Roman. *Iran: Parthians and Sasanians*. London, 1962.

Gignoux, Philippe. "Cachets sassanides du British Museum," pp. 125–48, in *Acta Iranica. Textes et Mémoires*. Vol. 5 Varia 1976. Téheran-Liège, 1977.

______. *Catalogue des Sceaux, camées et bulles sasanides de la Bibliothèque Nationale et du Musée du Louvre. II: Les Sceaux et Bulles Inscrits*. Paris, 1978.

Gignoux, Philippe, and Rika Gyselen. *Sceaux sasanides de diverses collections privées*. Cahiers de *Studia Iranica*, no. 1. Leuven, 1982.

______. *Bulles et Sceaux sasanides de diverses collections*. Cahiers de *Studia Iranica*, no. 4. Paris, 1987.

Göbl, Robert. *Der Sāsānidische Siegelkanon. Handbücher der mittelasiatischen Numismatik*, IV. Braunschweig, 1973.

Goodenough, Erwin R. *Jewish Symbols in the Greco-Roman Period*, Vols. II and III. Bollingen Series xxxvii. New York, 1953.

Graetz, Heinrich. *History of the Jews*, II. Philadelphia, 1893.

Grant, Michael. *The Jews in the Roman World*. New York, 1984.

Gropp, G. "Some Sasanian Clay Bullae and Seal Stones," pp. 119–44, in *The American Numismatic Society Museum Notes 19*. New York, 1974.

Gyselen, Rika. *Catalogue des sceaux, camées et bulles Sassanides. I. Collection générale*. Paris, 1982.

______. "Un vêtement masculin 'archaïsant' dans la glyptique sassanide (pl. 2)," pp. 39–44, in *Proceedings of the Third European Conference of Iranian Studies I. Old and Middle Iranian Studies*. Nicholas Sims-Williams, Editor. Wiesbaden, 1998.

Herzfeld, Ernst E. *Archaeological History of Iran*. London, 1935.

______. *Iran in the Ancient East: Archaeological Studies Presented in the Lowell Lectures at Boston*. London and New York, 1941.

Horn, Paul, and Georg Steindorff. *Sassanidische Siegelsteine*. Königliche Museen zu Berlin. Mitteilungen aus den orientalischen Sammlungen. IV. Berlin, 1891.

Hyman, Aaron. *Toledot tannel'im yd'elmora'im*, 1964, II: 553.

Kindler, Arie. "Lulab and Ethrog on a Seal in the Kadman Numismatic Museum," pp. 42–43, in *Museum Haaretz Bulletin 4*. June 1962.

Lerner, Judith. *Christian Seals of the Sasanian Period*. Uitgaven van het Nederlands Historisch-Archaeologisch Instituut te Istanbul, XLI. Istanbul, 1977.

Levine, Lee I. *The Ancient Synagogue: The First Thousand Years*. New Haven, Conn., and London, 1999.

Mordtmann, A. D. "Studien über geschnittene Steine mit Pehlevi-Inschriften," pp. 1–52, in *Zeitschrift der Deutschen morgenländischen Gesellschaft* 18. Leipzig, 1864.

Naveh, Joseph, and Shaul Shaked. *Amulets and Magic Bowls: Aramaic Incantations of Late Antiquity*. Jerusalem, 1985.

Neusner, Jacob. *A History of the Jews in Babylonia, V. Later Sasanian Times*. Leiden, 1970.

______ . *Judaism, Christianity, and Zoroastrianism in Talmudic Babylonia*. Lanham, Md., New York and London, 1986.

______ . *Israel and Iran in Talmudic Times: A Political History*. Lanham, Md., New York, and London, 1986.

Osten, H. H. von der. *Ancient Oriental Seals in the Collection of Mr. Edward T. Newell*. Oriental Institute Publications 22. Chicago, 1934.

Pope, Arthur U., and Phyllis Ackerman (eds.). *Survey of Persian Art*. Vols. 1 and 2. London and New York, 1938–39.

Roth, Cecil. *A History of the Jews*. New York, 1961.

Saggs, H. W. F. *Everyday Life in Babylonia and Assyria*. New York, 1965.

Shaked, Shaul. "Jewish and Christian Seals of the Sasanian Period," pp. 17–31 in *Studies in Memory of Gaston Wiet*. Myriam Rosen-Ayalon, Editor. Jerusalem, 1977.

______ . "Epigraphica Judaeo-Iranica," pp. 65–82, in *Studies in Judaism and Islam Presented to S. D. Goitein*. Jerusalem, 1981.

______ . "Jewish Sasanian Sigillography," pp. 239–55, in *Au Carrefour des Religions: Mélanges offerts à Philippe Gignoux*. Res Orientales VII. L'Institut français de recherche en Iran. Leuven, 1995.

Unvala, J. M. "Sassanian Seals and Sassanian Monograms," pp. 44–87, in *M. P. Khareghat Memorial Volume I*. Bombay, 1953.

Weitzman, Kurt, ed. *The Age of Spiritualism*. New York, 1979.

Widengren, Geo. "The Status of the Jews in the Sassanian Empire," pp. 117–62, in *Iranica Antiqua* I. Leiden, 1961.

______ . "The Status of Jews in the Sasanian Empire," in *Esther's Children: A Portrait of Iranian Jews*. Philadelphia, 2002.

Williams, Ron G., and James W. Boyd. *Ritual Art and Knowledge, Aesthetic Theory and Zoroastrian Ritual*. Columbia, S.C., 1993.

Wolfe, L. Alexander, and Frank Sternberg. *Objects with Semitic Inscriptions 1100 B.C.–A.D. 700. Jewish, Early Christian and Byzantine Antiquities*. Auction XXIII. Zurich, 1989.

Younger, J. G. *The Iconography of the Late Minoan and Mycenaean Sealstones and Finger Rings*. Bristol, England, 1988.

Index

DANIEL M. FRIEDENBERG is former curator of Coins and Medals for the Jewish Museum, New York. He is President of John-Platt Enterprises and a graduate of the Wharton School of Finance and Commerce. He is the recipient of the Heath Literary Award for Distinguished Numismatic Achievement and of the Loeb Magazine Special Achievement Award. He has been a contributing editor to *Dissent,* and is author of *Great Jewish Portraits in Metal, Jewish Medals from the Renaissance to the Fall of Napoleon, Medieval Jewish Seals from Europe,* and other books and articles.

The University of Illinois Press
is a founding member of the
Association of American University Presses.

Composed in 10.5/13.5 Minion Pro
by BookComp, Inc.
Manufactured by Thomson-Shore, Inc.

UNIVERSITY OF ILLINOIS PRESS
1325 South Oak Street Champaign, IL 61820-6903
www.press.uillinois.edu